The Collapse of Middle East Peace

The Collapse of Middle East Peace

✦

The Rise & Fall of the Oslo Peace Accords

Dennis J. Deeb II

iUniverse, Inc.
New York Lincoln Shanghai

The Collapse of Middle East Peace
The Rise & Fall of the Oslo Peace Accords

iUniverse, Inc.

For information address:
iUniverse, Inc.
2021 Pine Lake Road, Suite 100
Lincoln, NE 68512
www.iuniverse.com

ISBN: 0-595-29770-6

Printed in the United States of America

Dedicated to the late Israeli Prime Minister Yitzhak Rabin and all those who truly believe in the Oslo Peace Process and in reaching a lasting peace settlement between Israelis and Palestinians.

Contents

INTRODUCTION xi

CHAPTER 1   Brief Overview of the Palestinian-Israeli Conflict. 1

CHAPTER 2   Labor v. Likud: From Rabin to Sharon 8

CHAPTER 3   The Rise of Ariel Sharon & The Rejection of the
Oslo Accords 20

CHAPTER 4   Post-Oslo: The Mitchell Report & The U.S. Role
As Mediator. 32

CHAPTER 5   Palestinian Authority Reforms & The Quartet
Plan. 42

CONCLUSION. 49

APPENDIX A   The Oslo Agreement: Declaration Of Principles
On Interim Self-Government Arrangements 55

APPENDIX B   Text Of The Mitchell Report: Report Of The
Sharm El-Sheikh Fact-Finding Committee 71

APPENDIX C   United Nations Resolutions 242 and 338 Upon
Which The Oslo Agreements Were Based 101

APPENDIX D   QUARTET PLAN: Roadmap to a Permanent
Two-State Solution to the Israeli-Palestinian
Conflict 105

ENDNOTES 113

BIBLIOGRAPHY (RECOMMENDED READING) 129

ABOUT THE AUTHOR 131

ACKNOWLEDGMENTS

I would like to thank the following individuals for their assistance and support in critiquing and helping me to complete this work: *James K. Roth, Andrew James Gillon, John Hassan,* and *Professor Dean Bergeron.* Your friendship and guidance can never be repaid fully.

INTRODUCTION

The year 2002 seemed to offer little hope for a lasting peace in the Middle East and a settlement of the Israeli-Palestinian conflict. A new series of uprisings (Intifada) erupted in September 2000 following failed peace negotiations between the Israeli government of Ehud Barak and the Palestinian Authority as well as the visit by Israeli Likud Party Leader Ariel Sharon to the Temple Mount in Jerusalem. Just seven years earlier, the world watched in astonishment and joy as then Israeli Prime Minister Yitzhak Rabin and Palestine Liberation Organization [PLO] Leader Yasir Arafat signed a historic peace agreement, the Oslo Accords, in which both sides agreed to mutual recognition, security for Israel, self-rule for the Palestinians, and a dialogue regarding territorial compromise.

For more than fifty years, Israelis and Palestinians have strived to make significant gains and accomplishments at the expense of the other side. The primary purpose of the Oslo Peace Accords was to establish a process that would enable the Israelis and Palestinians to reach a Permanent Status Agreement based on peace, co-existence, and mutual recognition. The Oslo Accords allowed for all of the disputed issues between Israelis and Palestinians to be brought to the table, negotiated, and ultimately resolved.

From September 2000 to May 2003, more than 2,400 people, both Palestinians and Israelis, died in the fighting that had taken place. As of this writing, military curfews, economic isolation, air strikes, and tank bulldozing of villages are being used by the Israeli government against Palestinians while extremists on the Palestinian side are employing cruel acts of terrorism and suicide bombings against Israeli citizens.

In February 2001, Ehud Barak was overwhelmingly defeated by Ariel Sharon for Prime Minister. According to observers, Sharon had been plotting to achieve the post of Prime Minister since the mid-1980's. While campaigning, Sharon promised "peace with security." In announcing his intentions to run for Prime Minister, Sharon stated his purpose for running was to prevent further concessions to the Palestinians during the peace negotiations. In 1996, Sharon wrote of his disapproval and opposition to the Oslo Peace Process.

On the other side of the fighting, Palestinian Authority Leader Yasir Arafat has been unable or unwilling to control violent demonstrations and attacks by

Palestinians against Israeli citizens. Many Israelis also feel betrayed by the renewed round of terrorism and violence directed toward innocent civilians and the inability of the Palestinian Authority to stop the violence. Arafat has failed to halt Palestinian militants from making threats against Israel and spreading hostile propaganda in Palestinian media outlets. In addition, corruption and misman-agement on the part of the Palestinian Authority leadership, including Arafat, have also done much to stifle the Middle East peace process. Many Palestinians and outside observers have lost faith and confidence in Yasir Arafat's leadership and ability to forge a lasting agreement. Although on the surface, Arafat has appeared more willing to accept U.S.-sponsored peace proposals than the govern-ment of Ariel Sharon, his Palestinian Authority has presided over the collapse of the Palestinian economy despite receiving billions of dollars in aid from the inter-national community. This has called into question his ability to manage and maintain control over an independent Palestinian state. The Palestinian Author-ity needs to address its internal problems and reform its practices in order to demonstrate to the international community that it is capable to manage on behalf of the Palestinian people.

There are many issues facing both the Palestinians and the Israelis that need to be resolved. A glimmer of hope could be seen in May 2001 with the release of the much anticipated Mitchell Report. This report, generated by a panel led by former Maine Senator and Democratic Majority Party Leader George Mitchell, was prepared in response to an inquiry by the Clinton Administration. Previ-ously, Senator Mitchell had been successful in orchestrating a peace agreement in Northern Ireland. The Panel's recommendations will be discussed further on however, in summary, their recommendations were three-fold: 1) End the vio-lence; 2) Rebuild confidence; and 3) Resume negotiations. A follow-up to the Mitchell Report was released in the Spring of 2003 by President George W. Bush called the Quartet Plan Road Map To Peace. It is called the Quartet because input for the plan came from the United States, European Union, Russia, and the United Nations.

The age old conflict between the Israelis and the Palestinians is really a tragic tale of two peoples. Countless Israelis and Palestinian Arabs have lost their lives in conflict for causes they truly believed in. Many more have been killed or seriously injured because they just happened to be in the wrong place at the wrong time. I believe that a lasting peace agreement between both sides that guarantees the security of Israel, while acknowledging the right of self-determination and state-hood by the Palestinians, is in the best interests of both sides as well as in the interests of the world community.

The assassination of Prime Minister Yitzhak Rabin in 1994 and the subsequent events that followed marked the decline of the Middle East Peace Process and hopes for a lasting and comprehensive peace settlement between Israelis and Palestinians. Many Palestinians feel that they have been betrayed by Israel's leaders since Rabin's assassination.

Will Ariel Sharon bring a lasting peace and a comprehensive settlement between Israelis and Palestinians? A review of his past record of actions and statements affords a pessimistic response to those of us who believe in the spirit of the Oslo Peace Accords of 1993. Sharon has been a fierce and constant opponent of the Oslo Peace Process, the Mitchell Report, and even the Quartet Plan Road Map To Peace. He is considered a most controversial politician even within Israel. For the most part, Sharon is brutally forthright. He wants peace with security but on his terms. He wants peace without halting Israeli settlements in Palestinian areas and without territorial compromise. Palestinian leaders say and most observers agree that this is impossible. Thus, you have a collision course between Sharon and Palestinian leaders.

Sharon has a unique opportunity by the very nature of his position to bring lasting peace and security to Israel by compromising with the Palestinians. Mr. Sharon is absolutely right in insisting that security guarantees for Israel must be the priority, that reforms are needed within the Palestinian Authority, and that hostile actions by Palestinian militants must be halted. However, he is wrong in maintaining that the Palestinians do not have a right to self-determination, full statehood, and a right of return for Palestinian refugees.

The chapters that follow are intended to educate readers as to the rise and fall of the Oslo Peace Accords, the renewed Palestinian Uprising that began in September 2000, the actions taken by the Palestinian Authority, and the role of the current Israeli government of Prime Minister Ariel Sharon in these events and developments. In discussing these topics, I presented a brief, but by no means comprehensive, overview of the Israeli-Palestinian dispute. For a much more in-depth analysis of the Israeli-Palestinian and Israeli-Arab conflicts, I would suggest a reading of Thomas L. Friedman's best-selling book, *From Beirut To Jerusalem*. Friedman's book outlines the issues surrounding the whole Arab-Israeli conflict in a way that everyone can understand. I hope that this publication will inspire both Israelis and Palestinians to work to achieve a lasting peace settlement, rooted in the Oslo Peace Accords, and based on mutual recognition, respect, autonomy, and the peaceful co-existence of both Israel and an independent Palestinian State. The bulk of the writing contained in this work was written in 2000 and 2001. This manuscript was originally scheduled to be published in the Fall 2001. Following the horrific attacks of September 11, 2001, I withdrew this manuscript from planned publication because I felt the timing was not right to release a work of this nature. A great deal of activity has taken place since September 2001. As a result, I have updated and revised my original manuscript to include up-to-date information on the Israeli-Palestinian conflict through June 2003.

As of this writing, both the Israelis and the Palestinians have offered some positive reaction to the Mitchell Commission recommendations and President Bush's May 2003 Quartet Plan Road Map To Peace. These should serve as effective mechanisms for bringing the Palestinians and Israelis back to the table to negotiate a permanent peace settlement. Both sides will have to compromise. Both sides will have to give. Let us hope that both sides will seize the opportunity to achieve a lasting peace.

1

Brief Overview of the Palestinian-Israeli Conflict

Palestine was taken under the control of Great Britain following World War I and the collapse of the Ottoman Empire. The Balfour Declaration of 1917 supported the concept of a Jewish national home land in Palestine. Arab opposition against the creation of the State of Israel began to mount during this time.

The conflict between Palestinians and Israelis has its roots in the late nineteenth and the early twentieth century. During this time, Jewish settlers began to settle in Palestine. Many of these Jews were driven by a nationalist movement called Zionism. The Zionists encouraged Jews worldwide to settle in Palestine and to help create an independent Jewish state in that region. Most of the Jews who migrated to Palestine in the 1920's were motivated, skilled, and well-organized.[1] During the first part of the twentieth century, both Arab and Jewish settlers from Europe resided in Palestine. Thomas Friedman, a Pulitzer Prize-winning correspondent of *The New York Times*, wrote, "Most of the early Zionists either ignored the presence of the Arabs already in Palestine or assumed they could either be bought off or would eventually submit to Jewish domination."[2] As we know, the problem never disappeared but tensions only escalated in the years that followed.

At the end of World War II, tensions and fighting between Jewish settlers and Palestinian Arabs increased dramatically. It was during this time that the Zionist movement declared its intention of obtaining a dominant Jewish state in Palestine. In addition, after 1945, the Jewish underground, which consisted of a small minority of Jewish settlers, increased its campaign to oust the British from Palestine. The Jewish underground charged that the British had Arab sympathies. In order to achieve their objective, the Jewish underground initiated a series of terrorist attacks against the British.[3] Shortly afterwards, the British began to make plans to withdraw from the region, removing themselves from the political struggle for control.

In the fall of 1947, Great Britain, which had tried to work out an agreement between the Palestinian Arabs and the Jewish settlers, handed the problem over to the United Nations.

On November 29, 1947, the General Assembly of the United Nations voted thirty-three to thirteen to divide Palestine into two states—one Jewish and one Arab. The Jewish state would consist of the coastal plain between Tel Aviv and Haifa, northern Galilee, and the Negev Desert. The Palestinian Arab state would include the West Bank of the Jordan, the Gaza District, Jaffa, and the Arab regions of Galilee. Jerusalem, which was held most sacred by Jews, Muslims, and Christians was to be internationalized and placed under the trusteeship of the United Nations.

David Ben-Gurion, then leader of the Zionist Jewish movement, accepted this United Nations proposal however, the Palestinian Arabs and surrounding Arab countries completely rejected the proposal. Soon afterwards, the British peacekeepers, who had been present in Palestine since the end of World War I, announced their intention to leave the area by May 15, 1947.

On May 14, 1947, the Provisional State Council of Tel Aviv declared independence and the creation of a Jewish state in Palestine. Both the United States and the Soviet Union recognized Israel the same day it declared its independence. As a result, Israel's Arab neighbors stepped up their efforts to drive the Jews out of Palestine. The following day, military forces from Transjordan [now Jordan], Egypt, Lebanon, Syria, Saudi Arabia, and Iraq joined Palestinian guerillas in declaring war on the Jewish state. This constituted the first Arab-Israeli War and became Israel's War for Independence.

The Arab nations and the Palestinians were unsuccessful in preventing Israel from becoming an independent Jewish state. The Israelis defeated their Arab invaders and seized control of some Palestinian Arab territories as well. Following this defeat, Jordan annexed the West Bank and Egypt seized the Gaza District. Egypt and Jordan both refused to permit the Palestinian Arabs to form their own nation in these territories. A United Nations truce was reached which defined borders and frontiers for Israel which remained unaltered until the 1967 War.

Following the War for Israeli Independence, all Palestinians were granted full citizenship in Jordan. Soon afterwards, several other Arab countries granted partial or limited citizenship to Palestinians.

The new Jewish state came to occupy seventy-seven percent of the territory in Palestine. This resulted in the migration and expulsion of more than half of the

Palestinian Arab population. Since the West Bank and Gaza Strip, which was reserved for the Palestinian Arabs, was taken over by Egypt and Jordan, the Palestinian Arab state never came into being.[4] By the end of 1949, seven hundred thousand of the approximately nine hundred thousand Palestinian Arabs had fled their native Palestine as a result of terrorist attacks by the Jewish underground. The number of Jews in Palestine totaled about fifty thousand in 1917. By 1948, the Jewish population had increased to six hundred fifty thousand as a result of migration.

Throughout the 1950's tensions between Egypt and Israel increased dramatically. Egypt's president Gamel Abdel Nasser nationalized the Suez Canal which resulted in an Israeli attack on Egypt in 1956 with the assistance of Britain and France. During this attack, Egypt seized additional parts of the Gaza Strip and the Sinai Peninsula however, it later withdrew from Gaza and Sinai in 1957 following pressure from both the United States and the United Nations.[5]

The United Nations Security Council condemned Israel in 1951, 1953, 1955, and again in 1956 for attacking Palestinian villages under its control and for launching military attacks against surrounding Arab nations.[6]

Arab nationalism began to emerge after the 1956 war with Israel. This led to a united Arab military command that massed army troops along the borders with Israel.

These actions along with Egypt's closure of the Straits of Tiran resulted in the Israeli government simultaneously attacking Egypt, Jordan, and Syria on June 5, 1967. This war lasted six days and was a momentous victory for Israel. The Israelis seized the Gaza Strip and Sinai Peninsula from Egypt, Arab East Jerusalem and the West Bank from Jordan, and the Golan Heights from Syria. All of these occupied lands included an Arab population of approximately one and a half million people. This resulted in yet another exodus of Palestinians. On November 22, 1967, the United Nations adopted Resolution 242, which called on Israel to withdraw from the territories it had occupied in the 1967 conflict.

Egyptian President Gamal Abdel Nasser publicly stated his intentions to destroy the State of Israel following the 1967 War. During this time, Israel began employing Palestinian refugees in the West Bank and Gaza Strip. Many of these Palestinian workers labored for low wages and were afforded minimal benefits. This is still the case today in Israel. Israeli-occupation of the West Bank pushed more than four hundred thousand more Palestinians into neighboring Jordan.[7]

The Arab states created the Palestine Liberation Organization [PLO] in 1964. At first, its leaders were viewed as puppets of Egypt and Egyptian President Nasser. During this time, the PLO was extremist and largely disorganized. It received little recognition or backing from the Palestinian people. In 1969, a successful engineer, Yasir Arafat, became Chairman of the PLO. He enjoyed popular and widespread support from the Palestinian people and sought international recognition for the PLO.

Yasir Arafat was born in 1929 as one of seven children of a wealthy Palestinian merchant. Investigative reporter Thomas Friedman maintains that Arafat was able to keep the PLO independent and strong as a result of his skillful political maneuvering. Friedman writes, "Arafat did for the Palestinians what the Zionists did for the Jews: brought them from oblivion back into politics."[8]

Egypt and Syria attacked Israel on October 6, 1973 in an attempt to take back the areas lost in the 1967 war. This attack occurred on one of Israel's holiest days, Yom Kippur. For about three weeks, the Egyptian and Syrian forces seemed to be defeating the Israeli military. Military and financial assistance from the United States eventually helped Israel to fend off the Arab armies by October 24, 1973. United States Secretary of State Henry Kissinger was sent by President Richard Nixon to negotiate an agreement between Israel and Egypt in the Sinai and Israel and Syria in the Golan Heights in 1974.[9]

Palestinian guerilla forces had been operating out of Lebanon since 1978. These guerillas engaged in a series of attacks against Israel from the Lebanese border. On June 6, 1982, the Israeli military invaded Lebanon in an organized effort to destroy the PLO. Eight days later, both Syrian troops and the PLO forces were surrounded. They were forced to retreat to Syria in August. Soon afterwards, a cease-fire agreement was arranged and the PLO withdrew from Beirut and fled to neighboring Arab countries in exchange for security guarantees for thousands of Palestinian refugees left behind.[10] Thousands of Lebanese and Palestinian civilians were killed or injured following the 1982 conflict with Israel. These will be discussed further later on. By February 1985, the Israeli army withdrew from Lebanon however, it maintained a 'security zone' on the border. Border skirmishes continued between Palestinian guerillas and Israeli military forces throughout the 1980's.

Since 1967, Palestinians living in the Occupied Territories of the West Bank and Gaza Strip have been living under military authority. They are prohibited from voting, joining a labor unit, organizing politically, can be detained without formal charges, may be deported, and can have their property seized for Israeli settlements.[11]

An organized Palestinian revolt against Israeli-occupation, the Palestinian Intifada [uprising], began following an Israeli vehicle crash that killed four Palestinians on December 8, 1987. It first began in the Jebalya refugee camp in the Gaza

Strip to protest living conditions and treatment by Israeli authorities.[12] The Intifada lasted from 1987 to 1993 in the Israeli-occupied territories of the West Bank and Gaza Strip. The Uprising captured the attention and sympathy of much of the world community as hundreds of thousands of displaced Palestinian refugees took to the streets to protest what they viewed were deplorable living conditions and gross human rights violations at the hands of Israeli government authorities. The Intifada led to daily strikes and demonstrations by Palestinians, mostly youths, throwing stones and protesting physically in order to attract world attention to the Palestinian cause for self-determination.

In a June 1988 summit in Algiers, Arab nations officially recognized the PLO as the sole representative of the Palestinian people and Jordan's King Hussein renounced all claim to the West Bank which paved the way for the Palestinians to create their own independent state there if they could achieve a peace settlement with Israel.

In November 1988, the Palestine National Council, led by Yasir Arafat and the PLO, voted to accept the United Nations Resolutions 181 and 242 to accept the legitimacy of both a Jewish and Palestinian State. Resolution 181 acknowledged the right of Israel to exist as a sovereign nation and proposed that the City of Jerusalem be internationalized while Resolution 242 called on Israel to withdraw to its pre-1967 borders. In addition, the PLO formally renounced terrorism and endorsed negotiations to obtain a lasting settlement with the government of Israel.

Although many Palestinian citizens, including some PLO leaders, had said for years that they accepted a 'two-state' solution, encompassing both a Jewish and Palestinian state, to the Israeli-Palestinian conflict, it was not until 1988 that an official PLO declaration was made.[13] Following this declaration, the United States joined the rest of the world community in recognizing the PLO and engaging in dialogue with its leaders, including Arafat.

The Intifada began on the 70th anniversary of the British military conquest of Palestine. These demonstrators claimed that they had suffered long enough from the oppressive and inhumane treatment imposed on them for twenty-one years by Israeli government authorities.[14] The Palestinians living in the Israeli-occupied West Bank and Gaza Strip were clearly being treated as second class citizens.

Just before the beginning of the Intifada, the Israeli government had established an advanced computerized databank in the West Bank and Gaza Strip for the stated purpose of keeping track of every Palestinian's property, family history, political leanings, job occupation, licensing, consumption, and participation in illegal activities. West Bank expert Meron Benvenisti referred to this computerized databank as "the ultimate instrument of population control."[15]

When it began, the Intifada encompassed a completely unarmed Palestinian population that consisted of a mere one-third the size of the Israeli Jewish population. The Intifada caught the Israeli government by surprise.[16]

After the beginning of the Intifada, several Palestinians refused to pay taxes to the Israeli government. In response, the Israeli authorities announced that they were going to require all Palestinians to carry a new identity card in order to travel or hold a job. A condition for obtaining the new card was to pay all back taxes and to prove that no family member was wanted by the Israeli military. These actions made life even more difficult for countless Palestinians struggling to survive Israeli-occupation.

Seventy-five percent of the Palestinian population in the West Bank is under twenty-eight years old.[17] The Intifada ultimately served to empower Palestinian laborers, workers, and Palestinian youth.[18] United Nations correspondent Phyllis Bennett observed, "Israeli efforts to suppress the Intifada have included widespread collective punishment aimed at the entire population."[19] Collective punishment was outlawed by the 1949 Geneva Convention. Collective punishment serves only to foster more hatred and violence.

Thomas Friedman summarizes the underlying goal of many Palestinians in the Intifada. He writes, "The Palestinians must make themselves so indigestible to Israelis that they want to disgorge them into their own state, while at the same time reassuring the Israelis that they can disgorge them without committing suicide."[20]

At the November 15, 1988 meeting of the Palestine National Council in Algiers, Algeria, hundreds of Palestinian refugees and hundreds more newspaper reporters and media analysts gathered to hear the declaration of independence of the new nation of Palestine by PLO Chairman Yasir Arafat. This declaration was merely ceremonial since the rest of the world was not yet ready to recognize an independent Palestinian state.

During the first four years of the Intifada, more than one hundred hand grenade attacks and six hundred assaults with guns or explosives were reported by the government of Israel. The violence was directed at Israeli soldiers and Palestinians alike.[21]

Rioting and clashes between Palestinian protestors and Israeli troops continued in the early 1990's. The violence encompassed a continuation of stone-throwing and the use of homemade explosive devices on behalf of the Palestinians. Israeli troops utilized tear gas, rubber bullets, and home demolition in attempting to quell popular resistance.[22]

The Arab nations have to share some of the blame for the plight of the Palestinian people. As mentioned earlier, while controlling the West Bank and Gaza Strip, Jordan and Egypt refused to permit the formation of an independent Palestinian state.

2

Labor v. Likud: From Rabin to Sharon

All Israeli governments since Israel's founding in 1948 have been built on coalitions of several political parties since no single party has ever received enough seats in the Knesset, which serves as Israel's parliament, to form a government on its own. The government usually serves for eight years unless there is a resignation or death of a Prime Minister or if members of the Knesset pass a vote of no confidence.[1] The two major parties in the Israeli government are the Likud Party and the Labor Party.

The Israeli Labor Party is a socio-democratic party that has its roots in the Jewish labor movement. The Labor Party is pragmatic in its approach. The Platform reads, "The Labor Party has a principled commitment to the maintenance of a democratic form of government; to the enhancement of the social and economic well-being of all of Israel's citizens; to the strengthening of Israel's economy based on free market principles; and to the achievement of a comprehensive peace with security in the Middle East."[2] The Platform continues, "Israel's peace and security policy will be aimed toward ending the Israeli-Arab conflict." [3]

The Labor Party outlines its proposals for peace with the Palestinians on the basis of the Oslo Peace Accords as follows: JERUSALEM: United Jerusalem under Israeli sovereignty that allows Palestinian residents mutual rights; PALESTINIAN SELF-DETERMINATION: Recognizes right to self-determination by Palestinians and does not rule out the creation of an independent Palestinian state with limited sovereignty; SECURITY: The Jordan River will be Israel's eastern security border and there will be no other army stationed to the west of it; BORDERS AND SETTLEMENTS: Israel extends its sovereignty to areas that are major Jewish settlement blocs; THE RIGHT OF RETURN: Israel will negotiate with the Palestinians on allowing Palestinian refugees to return to areas under Palestinian control. In addition, the Labor Party Platform states that its leaders will continue to pursue a peace agreement with Syria and be open to compromise on the basis of land for peace. The Israeli Labor Party states that it is prepared to reach a peace agreement with an independent and sovereign Lebanon provided that any such agreements must include guarantees for security of both Israelis and Lebanese. The Labor Party Platform maintains that "The Oslo Agreements is based on the principles of mutual recognition and territorial compromise."[4] The Labor Party Platform concludes by claiming that the rival Likud Party seeks to ignore the Oslo Accords as the basis for further negotiations with the Palestinians. When considering prospects for peace between the Israelis and Palestinians, the Labor Party is certainly more reasonable and more likely to reach a permanent settlement with the Palestinians involving essential compromises on both sides.

The Labor Party leaders have a track record of reaching permanent and successful peace agreements with Israel's neighbors, namely Egypt and Jordan. Famous Labor Party leaders in Israel have included: David Ben-Gurion, Moshe Sharett, Levi Eshkol, Golda Meir, Moshe Dayan, Abba Eban, Yitzhak Rabin, Shimon Peres, and Ehud Barak.[5]

The Likud Party is less likely to successfully achieve peace with the Palestinians and Israel's other Arab neighbors since the Likud Party Platform supports the expansion of Jewish settlements in Palestinian areas and is committed to continuing to strengthen and develop these communities. The Likud Party also favors the renewal of peace negotiations with Syria without preconditions however, it also proposes to strengthen Jewish settlements on the Golan Heights.

The Likud Party has a completely different approach to dealing with the Palestinians from the more reasonable and moderate Labor Party. According to the Likud Platform, the Likud Party will insist that Palestinian Authorities institute the following policies: 1) A War on Terror; 2) Halting incitement against Israel; 3) Confiscation of illegal weapons; and 4) Reducing the size of the Palestinian Authority Police Force.

The Likud Party Platform "flatly rejects the establishment of a Palestinian Arab state west of the Jordan River."[6] Instead, the Likud Party proposes, "The Palestinians can run their lives freely in the framework of self-rule, but not as an independent and sovereign state."[7] The Likud Party Platform continues, "Thus, for example, in matters of foreign affairs, security, immigration, and ecology, their activity shall be limited in accordance with imperatives of Israel's existence, security, and national needs."[8]

The Likud Party further maintains that Jerusalem must remain the eternal, united capital of the state of Israel, and only of Israel, and that the Jordan River will be the permanent eastern border of the state of Israel.[9] Famous Likud Party leaders in Israel have included: Yitzhak Shamir, Benjamin Netanyahu, and Ariel Sharon. Most Likud Party leaders have presided over periods of violence and turmoil. Likud leaders are certainly reasonable in demanding security guarantees and full recognition of Israel's right to exist as a nation however, they too must be willing to make compromises to attain peace. This includes recognizing the Oslo Peace Accords, which were signed in Washington D.C. in 1993 and will be discussed more in detail further on. Netanyahu and Sharon have refused to recognize the Oslo Agreement and both have worked tirelessly to undermine its provisions.

In 1991, following the Persian Gulf War, peace talks began at Madrid between Israelis, Palestinians, Lebanese, Syrians, and Jordanians.

Between November 3 and November 9, 1991, the first round of bilateral discussions between Israeli and Palestinian authorities were held in Madrid, Spain. A second round of negotiations between Israeli and Palestinian authorities were held in Washington, D.C. from December 10-18, 1991. Little was accomplished in these discussions. Additional talks were held between Israelis and Palestinians between January 13-16, 1992 in Washington, D.C. Israel's Likud Party Leader and Prime Minister Yitzhak Shamir and his delegation presided over these talks.

On June 23, 1992, Yitzhak Rabin was elected Prime Minister. Rabin's election would change the course of history. Rabin envisioned a lasting peace settlement between Israelis and Palestinians. Rabin was a true visionary and man of peace who translated words and ideas into positive action.

Yitzhak Rabin served as Israel's Prime Minister from 1974 to 1977 and again from 1992 to 1995. His latter term concerns us here. In 1992, Rabin defeated Shimon Peres for leadership of Israel's Labor Party and then as Prime Minister however, Rabin later appointed Peres as his Foreign Minister. Rabin was born on March 3, 1922 to Roza and Nehemya Rabin. While in high school, Rabin joined the Palmach part of the Israeli army to fight for Israeli independence from Britain.[10]

Rabin's policies and goals from 1992 to 1995 included withdrawing most of Israeli military forces from Lebanon, signing a peace accord with Jordan, and engaging in formal dialogue with the PLO.[11]

Rabin campaigned for and was elected on a platform of peace that included coming to a swift agreement on Palestinian autonomy. Rabin did not intend to settle the final status of the territories, however, he would begin the long process of resolving the century-old dispute between Palestinians and Israelis.

Rabin signed the Oslo Peace Agreement with PLO Leader Yasir Arafat on September 13, 1993 in Washington, D.C. The agreement was originally negotiated at Oslo, Norway. In signing the agreement, Rabin remarked, "enough of the blood and tears."[12] The Oslo Peace Accords provided for mutual recognition between Israel and the PLO and for limited self-rule for the Palestinians in the Palestinian territories of Jericho and Gaza. The Agreement also stated that the Israeli government acknowledges the PLO as the sole Palestinian Authority, the legitimate representative of the Palestinian people. In return, the PLO promised to crack down on terrorism and acknowledged the existence of the State of Israel and the right of that nation to exist in peace and security. At that time, the Agreement was seen as an intermediate first step toward the creation of an independent Palestinian State.

The Declaration of Principles of the Interim Self-Government Agreement, which was incorporated into the Oslo Agreement, reads that the Government of the State of Israel and the PLO team acknowledges that their peoples must "strive to live in peaceful coexistence and mutual dignity and security and achieve a just, lasting, and comprehensive peace settlement and historic reconciliation through the agreed political process."[13] The Oslo Accords established the aim of negotiations and a framework for an interim period. It also established a time frame for elections in the Palestinian areas of the West Bank and Gaza Strip, economic collaboration, withdrawal of Israeli troops from the Jericho and Gaza Strip areas, and security guarantees for Israel.[14]

The Oslo Peace Accords of 1993 specified the following arrangements:

1. **A Palestinian Government**

2. **A Palestine Council with free elections**

3. **Voting rights for Palestinians**

4. **Limits on Council Authority**

5. **Israeli troop withdrawal**

6. **A strong Palestinian police force**

7. **A 5-year transition period**

8. **Negotiations based on United Nations Resolutions 242 and 338 leading to their implementation**

9.   **Discussions on Palestinian refugees**

10. **Talks regarding the status of Jerusalem.**[15]

U.N. Resolution 242 passed on November 22, 1967, called on Israel to with-draw to its pre-1967 borders and for neighboring Arab states to acknowledge Israel's sovereignty. Resolution 338, passed on October 22, 1973, called on Israel and its Arab neighbors to implement Resolution 242 and begin negotiations aimed at establishing a permanent peace settlement in the region.

In promoting the Oslo Peace Accords, Rabin wrote, "Wars have their victors and their vanquished, but everyone is a victor in peace."[16] Journalist Jonathan Parker wrote, "Mr. Rabin was elected Prime Minister in 1992 and in three years came closer to peace than anyone else could have in 47 years."[17] The Intifada Uprising officially ended in 1993 following the signing of the Oslo Peace Accords.

In May 1994, another follow-up agreement, known as the Cairo Accords, was signed by Israel and the PLO in Cairo, Egypt. This agreement provided for:

1.   **A scheduled withdrawal of Israeli military forces from Gaza and Jericho**

2.   **Transfer of limited governance to the Palestinian Authority**

3.   **Established a structure and composition of the Palestinian Authority**

4.   **Established the legislative powers and responsibilities of the Palestinian Authority**

5.   **An arrangement for security and public order**

6.   **A Palestinian police force**

7.   **Safe passage between the Gaza Strip and Jericho**

8.   **Diplomatic relations between Israel and the Palestinian Authority**

9.   **A liaison and cooperation between Egypt and Jordan**

10. **Settlement of disputes and prevention of hostile acts between the parties**

11. **Confidence building measures and a temporary international presence in Gaza and Jericho**

12. **An acknowledgement of rights, liabilities, and obligations of both parties.**[18]

Under this agreement, a twenty-four member Palestinian National Authority, appointed by the PLO and headed by Yasir Arafat, governs the region, makes its laws, and is in charge of its economic policies. However, the Israelis retained most of the security authority and were responsible for the frontier areas and buffer zones around Israeli settlements. This agreement was seen as another step in the movement toward complete Palestinian self-rule of this area and the whole West Bank. Additional agreements providing for a transfer of control to the Palestinians of other West Bank towns and the complete Gaza Strip were finalized in 1994 and 1995. These were all based upon the Oslo Accords. Under the terms of the Oslo Accords, the Palestinian Authority is obligated to refrain from incitement against Israel and to take measures to prevent others from engaging in it.

In a letter to Rabin following the signing of the Oslo Accords, Arafat wrote that the PLO recognizes the right of the State of Israel to exist in peace and security. In addition, Arafat wrote that the PLO accepts United Nations Security Council Resolutions 242 and 338.[19] As explained earlier, these Resolutions called on Israel to withdraw to its 1967 borders. The September 9, 1993 letter read, "The PLO renounces the use of terrorism and other acts of violence and will assume responsibility over all PLO elements and personnel in order to ensure their complete compliance, prevent violations, and discipline violators."[20]

Because of these historic agreements, Rabin and Arafat both would receive the Nobel Peace Prize along with future Prime Minister Shimon Peres the following year. On October 26, 1994, Rabin also signed a historic peace agreement with King Hussein of Jordan.

On September 28, 1995, Rabin participated in the signing of the Oslo B. Article XXII of the Oslo B Interim Agreement of September 28, 1995 states that Israel and the Palestinian Authority "shall seek to foster mutual understanding and tolerance and shall accordingly abstain from incitement, including hostile propaganda, against each other and, without derogating from the principle of freedom of expression, shall take legal measures to prevent such incitement by organizations, groups, or individuals within their jurisdiction."[21]

On Saturday, November 4 of the same year, following his attendance at a peace rally in Tel Aviv, Rabin was shot and killed by Igala Meir, a twenty-five-year-old Israeli extremist and law student who opposed the Oslo Accords. Following the assassination, Meir was questioned as to his motivation for killing Rabin. Meir replied, "I was opposed to the peace process."[22]

The National Alliance of Lebanese Americans, in an editorial position statement released just days after Rabin's assassination, observed that "the Israeli
Prime Minister became a victim of his own peace policy when he was gunned
down by a fellow Israeli."[23] The Paper asserted that prior to Rabin's election, the
Israeli-Palestinian Peace talks were going nowhere. It credited Rabin with establishing a new precedent for Israel that encompassed an agenda of peace with the
Palestinians and its Arab neighbors.[24] On November 22, 1995, just thirteen days
following Rabin's assassination, Peres was appointed by the Israeli Knesset as acting Prime Minister and Defense Minister. He held these two positions until the
spring elections. Shimon Peres was born in Poland in August 1923. He moved to
Tel Aviv with his family in 1934. In 1953, Peres was appointed as Director General of the Defense Ministry by then Prime Minister David Ben-Gurion. Peres
was elected to the Knesset in 1959. Peres is married and is the father of three children.

As mentioned earlier, Peres was the recipient of the Nobel Peace Prize in
1994, along with Arafat and Rabin, for his efforts in helping to negotiate the
Oslo Peace Accords.[25] During Peres' short tenure as Prime Minister, a series of
terrorist attacks and suicide bombings by Palestinians were targeted against Israel
by Palestinian extremists and militants opposed to the peace process. These militants claimed that the peace process was not moving along fast enough. These
actions and developments made it difficult for significant advancements to be
made.[26] Peres found himself in a very difficult and complicated situation.

In early 1996, Yasir Arafat was elected President of the Palestinian-controlled
territory. Arafat wasted no time in taking control and in exercising the authority
awarded him under the Oslo Peace Accords. His jurisdiction encompassed designated portions of the West Bank and Gaza Strip.

In May 1996, Israeli Likud Party Leader Benjamin Netanyahu, an outspoken
critic of the Oslo Peace Accords, narrowly defeated Peres and was elected Israel's
new Prime Minister. Netanyahu became Israel's ninth and youngest Prime Minister at thirty-seven years old. He won 50.5% of the popular vote compared to
Peres' 49.5%. Netanyahu campaigned promising the eradication of terrorism and
the establishment of peace. He is the author of numerous books on terrorism and
Israel's security Benjamin Netanyahu was born on October 21, 1949. He is married and is the father of three children. He received the bulk of his education in
the United States, attending high school in Philadelphia and receiving a degree
from Harvard University and Massachusetts Institute of Technology.

Benjamin Netanyahu had been an outspoken critic of the peace process and
gained a reputation for saying what he thought regardless of public opinion. In

campaigning for Prime Minister, Netanyahu promised to undo whatever steps had been taken toward peace with the Palestinians as resembled in the Oslo Agreements. According to *CNN*, after being elected Prime Minister, Benjamin Netanyahu "adopted an unwavering stance which did little to further the peace process." [27] Netanyahu himself wrote in a 1994 book, "If there is to be peace, it will have to mean, at long last, the recognition of Palestinian Arabs that they are in the minority in the forty miles west of the Jordan River, and they will receive no additional independent states there."[28] Netanyahu's agenda as Prime Minister encompassed the expansion of Israeli settlements in Palestinian areas and maintaining the territory of Israel as it was with no territorial concessions to the Palestinians.[29] On October 17, 1996, Netanyahu cancelled the Labor government's freeze, instituted by Rabin and Peres, on Israeli construction in Palestinian territories while announcing plans to expand existing Israeli settlements and build new roads and industrial parks throughout the West Bank and Gaza Strip.[30] In his book, *A Durable Peace*, Netanyahu had argued that the Palestinians should settle for self-determination within Israeli jurisdiction rather than demand a completely independent state of their own.[31] Netanyahu's actions and policies increased tensions with and angered Palestinians.

Under Netanyahu's reign, violence escalated among Palestinian protesters who felt that the mission of Netanyahu's policies were intended to undermine the Oslo Peace Accords, which he continued to oppose throughout his term. The Wye River Accords of 1998 offered a dim shade of hope for the Palestinians. The Wye River Conference between Netanyahu and Arafat was held in Maryland and was mediated by Jordan's King Hussein and President Bill Clinton. This established that the Palestinians would erase from their founding charter language that called for the destruction of the Jewish state. In return, the Netanyahu government transferred an additional thirteen percent of the West Bank to Palestinian self-rule. In addition, the deadline of September 13, 2000 was agreed on to establish a final peace agreement. This calmed some of the tensions by Palestinians but, many of the Palestinians were still very upset with the continuation of Israeli expansion settlements in the occupied territories.[32]

On May 17, 1999, Ehud Barak, a member of the Knesset and Labor Party leader, defeated Benjamin Netanyahu and became Israel's tenth Prime Minister. Netanyahu had not only been criticized by the West for his stances with the Palestinians, he had also been attacked for his internal policies. Scandals plagued Netanyahu's government toward the latter part of his term. Ehud Barak was born in 1942 on a kibbutz that his parents helped found near the Lebanese border. Barak campaigned for Prime Minister as a centrist who supported the Peace Process with the Palestinian Authority. Barak promised to reach a final peace settlement with the Palestinians and also hinted at a territorial compromise involving the Golan Heights with Syria in exchange for peace.[33]

Barak had a long history of involvement in the Israeli Military and in the politics of his country. He had a distinguished military career from the time he joined the Israeli Defense Forces in 1959. In January 1982, Barak was appointed Head of the IDF Military Planning Branch and promoted to Major General. In April 1983, Barak was appointed Head of the Intelligence Branch at the IDF General Headquarters. In 1994, Barak was awarded the "Distinguished Service Medal" for his courageous military service. After serving in the Israeli military for thirty-five years in 1995, Barak retired as Army Chief of Staff and joined the Labor Party. He served briefly as Interior Minister under Rabin and as Foreign Minister under Peres. In 1996, Barak was elected to the Knesset. Later that year, he was elected Chairman of the Labor Party.

Extensive talks and negotiations between Barak and the Palestinian Authority took place during his tenure as Prime Minister, however, little was accomplished with regards to a permanent peace settlement involving territorial compromise. Toward the end of President Bill Clinton's term of office in the fall of 2000, the two sides came to a complete standstill in the negotiations held at Camp David over territorial concessions, Israeli settlement expansions, and the right of return for Palestinian refugees. Talks were also stalled over the status of Jerusalem.[34] Much was written about these events in the national and international news. The Israeli government claimed that Arafat was demanding too much and that Barak was offering the Palestinian Authority a comprehensive package that was fair and consistent with the spirit of the Oslo Accords.

The Palestinians argued that they could not accept Barak's proposal for three reasons: 1) The territory offered was scattered and the way it was configured would make a Palestinian state virtually impossible; 2) United Nations Resolution 242 called for Israel to withdraw to its 1967 borders and this was the spirit of Oslo. In their acceptance of Oslo, Palestinians accepted a two-state solution and this was a compromise of over half of the area that was originally assigned to them; and 3) The Barak offer stemmed from the continued illegal occupation, confiscation, and expropriation of Palestinian land.[35]

Other observers pointed out, "Barak's coalition was not very trustworthy...The ultraorthodox shas-Party blackmailed the government to satisfy the demands of its clientele."[36] The shas-Party was opposed to the Oslo Peace Accords as well as any land-for-peace settlement. To further complicate matters, more illegal Israeli settlements were constructed in occupied Palestinian areas under Barak than under any other Israeli Prime Minister.

The negotiations also broke down at Camp David between Barak and Arafat largely over the failure of the parties to reach an agreement on the right of refugees to return to Palestinian territories. The Palestinians want to secure the rights of some four million Palestinian refugees worldwide to return to an independent Palestinian state.

Professor Elaine C. Hagopian of Simmons College wrote in a *Boston Globe* column, "Final status negotiations were set in July 2000 at Camp David. Arafat was told to sign away Palestinian rights to fully sovereign statehood and refugee return. Having given in to US-Israeli pressure on interim agreements, his refusal to sign was interpreted as some sort of ploy. The so-called concessions by Barak had two problems: As an occupying power, 'concessions' were not Israel's to make; and close examination of the 'generous concessions' announced in the media show the profile of bantustans choked by Israeli settlements, roads, and border controls."[37]

Professor Hagopian continues, "The Jerusalem 'concessions' were all fluff, no substance. In return, Barak expected Arafat to be complicit in denying the inalienable rights of Palestinian refugees, 70 percent of the Palestinian population."[38]

Robert Malley, who served as Special Assistant to President Clinton for Arab-Israeli Affairs, was a member of the U.S. peace team and participated in the summit at Camp David, claimed that the Israelis and Palestinians each came to Camp David with very different perspectives which complicated the discussions. Malley confirms that Barak's wavering and lack of leadership skills contributed significantly to the collapse of the Camp David Peace Talks. Malley writes, "To begin, Barak discarded a number of interim steps, even those to which Israel was formally committed by various agreements—including a third partial redeployment of troops from the West Bank, the transfer to Palestinian control of three villages abutting Jerusalem, and the release of Palestinians imprisoned for acts committed before the Oslo Agreement...Oslo was being turned on its head."[39] One of Barak's own government Ministers, Haim Ramon, stated in a March 2, 2001 interview, "Ehud was actually against Oslo; his government abandoned the path for peace."[40] To achieve a lasting peace, Israelis and Palestinians must implement the provisions of the Mitchell Report and acknowledge the previously-signed Oslo Peace Accords as a foundation for reaching a final and comprehensive peace settlement.

Former U.S. Ambassador Martin Indyk has blamed both Palestinian and Israeli leaders for failing to reach a permanent peace settlement. Indyk has stated further that he does not expect a permanent peace settlement to be reached any-time in the foreseeable future.[41] This represents a severe setback and a sad state of affairs for Israelis and Palestinians. Both sides need to come to terms with each other, put aside their differences and the violence, implement prior agreements, and negotiate a final settlement that guarantees security and autonomy for both sides.

It was further reported that in attempting to secure a peace accord, the Barak government had offered to hand over about ninety-five percent of the West Bank and all of Gaza, a division of Jerusalem, and the removal of some Israeli settle-ments from Palestinian areas.[42] This information, as reported in many leading news media outlets, is incorrect according to Rachelle Marshall of the Interna-tional Jewish Peace Union. According to Marshall, the offer Barak made to the Palestinians "was far short of what they could accept. The map [offered by Israel] showed the settlement blocs that Barak insisted upon annexing to Israel extend-ing like thick fingers across the West bank from Jerusalem to Jericho...What remained to the Palestinians would be three segments of land, each one sur-rounded by Israeli settlements and roads."[43] Marshall observed, "Barak was hailed in the American press for his willingness to relinquish more territory than any previous prime minister, but his plan would nevertheless have allowed Israel to maintain its grip on the West Bank."[44] New York University Professor Lev Grinberg has claimed that Barak went to Camp David with the support of only twenty-five percent of the Knesset, knowing that a chance for a settlement was impossible in order to create the myth that a generous offer had been proposed by Israel to the Palestinian Authority.[45]

By the fall and winter of 2000, Barak came under heavy criticism for his poor political skills, lack of effective diplomacy, and inability to end the violence.[46] In addition, Barak worked to expand Jewish settlements in Palestinian areas, con-tinuing the expansion policies of his predecessor, Netanyahu.[47] Violence erupted in late September following a visit by Likud Party Leader Ariel Sharon and his delegation to the Temple Mount, the most sacred religious site to both Jews and Moslems. Reportedly, Sharon, who visited the site armed, had made some con-troversial remarks regarding the peace process and the status of Jerusalem in the talks. This, along with the failure for a peace agreement to be reached by Barak and Arafat, sparked a new wave of violence against Israel by Palestinian protest-ors, Intifada II, which had not been seen since the signing of the Oslo Peace Accords in September 1993. Barak was widely viewed as a weak leader because he had also failed to adequately address domestic issues since crime and unemployment soared during his administration.[48] In February 2001, Barak would lose his position as Prime Minister to Ariel Sharon. This will be the subject of the next chapter.

3

The Rise of Ariel Sharon & The Rejection of the Oslo Accords

On November 28, 2000, the Israeli Knesset voted overwhelmingly to dissolve itself which paved the way for early elections for Prime Minister to be scheduled in February 2001. At that point in time, Barak had served as Prime Minister for just a year and a half. In Israel's February 6, 2001 election, Ariel Sharon defeated Ehud Barak 62.5% to 37.4% in the election for Prime Minister. Sharon won his election over Barak in the lowest voter turnout in Israeli history. Sixty-two percent of eligible Israelis voted compared to the average turnout of eighty percent. Sharon had been considered one of Israel's most controversial military and political leaders. He too had an extensive military and political career prior to assuming his new position. Sharon was previously serving as Chairman of Israel's Likud Party. He was viewed as a hardliner in Israeli politics and was an outspoken critic of the Oslo Peace Accords. In campaigning for Prime Minister, Sharon had promised "peace with security."[1]

Sharon had announced his intentions to run against Prime Minister Ehud Barak in the February 2001 elections on November 28, 2000, the same day that the Israeli Knesset voted to dissolve itself. In making his announcement, Sharon stated his purpose for running was to halt what he viewed as further concessions to the Palestinians in peace negotiations. Sharon argued against a final peace agreement encompassing an exchange of land for peace. Instead, Sharon proposed an interim pact on what he called non-belligerence. At that time, a Likud Party challenge was expected from former Prime Minister Benjamin Netanyahu, however, a procedural clause in Israel's parliamentary government ended up preventing Netanyahu's candidacy. Sharon claimed that he liked Barak personally but that, Barak lacked political experience and was thus incapable of finalizing a long-term peace agreement with the Palestinians. It is perhaps worth mentioning that Ehud Barak was given the rank of brigadier-general of the Israeli army by

Sharon decades earlier.[2] Sharon had stated, "I am for a lasting peace…I believe that I understand the importance of peace better than many of the politicians who speak about peace but never had that experience. For me, peace should provide security to the Jewish people and peace for generations."[3]

Before discussing Sharon's political views, it is important to first understand his background and upbringing. Sharon was born in 1928. He joined the Israeli Haganah at an early age.[4] Haganah was an underground Jewish military resistance organization.[5] At age eighteen, Sharon fought in the war for Israeli independence against Great Britain.[6] Sharon had first enlisted in the Israeli resistance of British-ruled Palestine at age fourteen.[7]

In 1948, Sharon commanded an intelligence unit in the Israeli army during the first Israeli-Palestinian war. During the 1950's, Sharon commanded the elite Commando Unit 101 of the Israeli Army.[8] In 1956, Sharon acted beyond orders in commanding the Israeli army during the Suez-Sinai War. His actions resulted in many more casualties on the Israeli side, however, Sharon's victories against the Palestinians and Arabs made him a national hero at home.

Following the 1967 Six-Day War, Sharon served as military commander of the Gaza Strip. During this time, twenty-four hour curfews on civilians were instituted and an intense harassment of Palestinian citizens followed.[9] As brigadier general and division commander during the Six Day War in June 1967, Sharon was instrumental in capturing East Jerusalem, the West Bank, and the Gaza Strip.[10]

In 1973, Sharon successfully commanded a division in the Yom Kippur War. He then left the Army to enter Israeli politics. Sharon was later active in the formation of the Likud Party. In December 1973, Sharon was elected to the Israeli Knesset.

Sharon is not that tall in stature. He stands at approximately five feet eight inches. He was born Ariel Schoenerman and took the name Sharon, meaning "lion" after then Prime Minister David Ben-Gurion, ordered that all Israeli soldiers adopt Hebrew names. The name Ariel Sharon means "Lion of God" in Hebrew.[11]

Sharon attended the Comberley Staff College in Great Britain in 1957. He attended law school at Tel Aviv University during the early 1960's. Sharon's family life has encompassed more than its share of tragedy. Sharon's first wife, Margalit, died in a car accident in the early 1960's. According to biographer Uzi Benziman, Sharon was deeply affected by her death.[12] A year after Margalit's death, Sharon married his wife's sister Lilly and had two more sons.[13] Lilly had previously lived in the Sharon household for a period of time, however, tensions had grown between her and Margalit.[14] Sharon's oldest son was killed years before while playing with a loaded gun in Sharon's home. Sharon was again struck by tragedy in 2000 when Lilly died of cancer.

In 1974, Sharon resigned as a member of the Knesset in order to assume a senior emergency position in the Israeli military reserves. Soon afterwards, Sharon became an advisor to then Prime Minister Yitzhak Rabin. In 1976, Sharon was instrumental in the founding of the ultra-right Schlomzian Party. The following year, the Schlomzian Party won two seats in the Israeli Knesset. Sharon later joined Schlomzian with the Likud Party and became Minister of Agriculture. As Agriculture Minister, Sharon took steps to improve relations with Egypt. He opened the southern border for Egyptians wishing to visit Israel and he offered to permit Egyptian ships to use Israeli port facilities. Sharon writes of serving with Rabin, "I stayed with Rabin from June 1975 to February 1976, by which time I decided I had learned everything I was going to and had made all the contributions I could."[15] Sharon continued, "When I entered the government as minister of agriculture, I felt almost as if I was coming home. Farming was in my blood, and Israel's large agriculture sector presented an array of interesting and difficult problems."[16] Sharon proudly proclaims that as Minister of Agriculture, he worked to rapidly expand Israeli settlements in the West Bank.[17]

Sharon supported the Camp David Peace Accords with Egypt in 1979, negotiated by Egyptian President Answar Sadat and Israeli Prime Minister Menachim Begin with the support and assistance of President Jimmy Carter. Sharon explains, "I had supported the Camp David Accords because I believed that after all those years of bloodshed we had an obligation to see if there was any possibility for peaceful coexistence."[18] He continues, "In essence, the Camp David plan called for a balance between 'the principle of self-government' for the Palestinians and 'the legitimate security concerns' of the Israelis."[19] According to Benziman, Prime Minister Begin refused to appoint Sharon as Minister of Defense because he feared that one of his first moves would be to surround government offices with military tanks.[20]

Sharon was eventually appointed Defense Minister in 1981. As Minister of Defense, he had the following objectives: 1) To remove Israeli settlements in the Northern Galilean region from the range of terrorist attacks; 2) To crush the Palestinian resistance in Lebanon; 3) To establish a legitimate government in Lebanon that would sign a peace accord with Israel; and 4) To accomplish the withdrawal of Syrian military forces from Beirut. For the most part, these goals were accomplished by January 1982.[21] The following year, he led an Israeli attack mission in Lebanon which encompassed a military operation to defeat Palestinian guerilla forces in and around the capital city of Beirut. The stated mission of Sharon's invasion was the destruction of the Palestine Liberation Organization [PLO]. Sharon successfully occupied Beirut and forced the PLO out of Lebanon. The PLO evacuated and moved their forces to Tunis. The mission lasted several weeks and Sharon also presided over the killings of two thousand Palestinian and Lebanese refugees outside Beirut by a Lebanese Christian militia. Sharon came under heavy criticism for his actions by both the Israeli public and by the international community. Several months later, Sharon was forced to resign his position as Defense Minister after an Israeli investigation committee, the Kahan Commission, ruled him indirectly responsible for the killings and thus, unfit to be Defense Minister. In conducting his mission, according to researcher Jeremy Salt, "Sharon launched attacks aimed at the heavily populated capital of Beirut, destroying apartment buildings, orphanages and hospitals, along with civilian encampments."[22] In his autobiography, Sharon responds, "As I told them [Israeli government officials] in the cabinet meeting, by accepting the Kahan Commission report they themselves had put the mark of Cain not only on my forehead but on that of the Jewish people and the state of Israel."[23]

Time magazine was one of the first news outlets to report on Sharon's activities in Lebanon. Sharon filed a lawsuit against *Time* for what he claimed was sensational journalism. The specifics of the lawsuit are documented in a book by Uri Dan called *Blood Libel: The Inside Story of General Ariel Sharon's History-Making Suit Against Time Magazine*. *Time* alleged that Sharon had held secret meetings with Lebanese leaders prior to the massacre and that the incident was actually planned. Sharon responded that this allegation "was a complete lie."[24] Sharon ended up losing his lawsuit against *Time* and blamed his defeat on the shortcomings of the American judicial system.[25]

In his autobiography, *Warrior*, Ariel Sharon writes of his childhood, military, political career, and his family history. Sharon believes strongly that Israel must act independently of the United States.[26]

Sharon proclaims, "I am looking forward to the day when there will be peace between the Jews and the Arabs. And personally I believe that in order to have this peace the Palestinians need a political expression."[27] However, Sharon claims later in his autobiography that Trans-Jordan, now Jordan, was originally intended to be the homeland for the Palestinian people.[28] Sharon maintains that withdrawal from [Palestinian] territories will only create more violence and cause a greater threat to Israel's security.[29] By opposing the creation of an independent Palestinian state, Sharon will not be able to bring about a lasting peace or security for Israel.

Ariel Sharon's biggest critics include left-wing Israelis and Palestinians. *BBC News* Correspondent and Middle East Analyst Gerald Butt writes, "Ariel Sharon has thick skin and is proud of it. He does not care who loves him or who hates him—be they Israelis or Arabs. The one aim in life for the 72-year old former soldier and veteran politician is to ensure total security for Israel on his own terms."[30] *CNN* points out, "To his right-wing supporters, Sharon is a war hero who will stand tough to protect Israeli interests against hostile Arab neighbors. To Palestinians and dovish Israelis, he is a bulldozer in a China shop, someone who will kill what's left of the peace process."[31] Sharon views himself as a pragmatist. He told *CNN*, "I believe in peace, but I believe in peace that might provide Israel with real security for its existence."[32]

Ariel Sharon argues that since the Arab nations initially rejected United Nations General Assembly Resolution No. 181 of November 1947, which proposed that the City of Jerusalem be internationalized, the issue of Jerusalem was settled by the wars that followed in which Israel was the victor. Sharon maintains that Jerusalem will remain the united eternal capital of Israel and is not a subject for negotiation.[33]

Sharon has further cautioned that Israel should not be pressured to reach a peace agreement with Syria. He has argued against the return of the Golan Heights on the following grounds: 1) There must be no rewards for the aggressor; 2) National defense requires territory; 3) Syrian armed forces must be reduced; and 4) Comprehensive peace must also include measures to contain Iraq and Iran which are amassing a stockpile of dangerous weapons. Sharon editorialized in *The New York Times* in 1999, "I believe Israel must keep the Golan Heights."[34]

Sharon was a fierce opponent of engaging in negotiations with the PLO. In his best-selling book, *From Beirut to Jerusalem*, Thomas Friedman claims that by invading Beirut, Sharon was hoping to force the one point seven million Palestinians living in the West Bank and Gaza Strip to abandon their pursuit of an independent Palestinian state by destroying their representative, the Palestine Liberation Organization [PLO], and accepting limited autonomy granted by Israel. This would allow Israel to forever retain control over the West Bank and Gaza.[35]

In 1984, Sharon sought out to become the new leader of the Likud Party and his attempts were unsuccessful since he lost the election. In September of that year, he was appointed Minister of Trade and Industry by then Prime Minister Shimon Peres. Sharon served in that position until 1990.

In early 1990, Sharon resigned from his position as Minister of Trade and Industry. Shortly afterwards, the government of Shimon Peres was overthrown.

Yitzhak Shamir was elected Israel's new Prime Minister in May 1990. Shamir appointed Sharon to be Minister of Housing. During this time, Sharon worked to rapidly accelerate Jewish settlements in the occupied West Bank and Gaza Strip.

In 1992, with the defeat of the Likud Party and Prime Minister Yitzak Shamir's coalition government and with the election of Yitzhak Rabin as the Labor Party Prime Minister, Sharon resigned as Minister of Housing. From 1992 to 1997, Sharon was virtually absent from Israeli government positions with the administrations of Rabin and Shimon Peres.[36] During this time, Sharon became a very vocal statesman and activist for the Likud Party. He railed against the peace negotiations between the Labor Government and the PLO and strongly opposed the Oslo Peace Accords.

Shortly after the election of Benjamin Netanyahu as Prime Minister in 1996, Netanyahu appointed Sharon Minister of Agriculture. It was reported that in May 1997, Sharon proposed annexing large portions of the West Bank to provide additional water resources for Israeli citizens. The concept was raised and discussed at a secret meeting of Israeli government officials. During this time, Palestinians controlled twenty-seven percent of the West Bank. They maintained that in accordance with the Oslo Peace Accords, Israel must hand over more than ninety percent as part of peace agreements already signed. Under Sharon's proposal Israel would have maintained control over water resources even in areas under Palestinian control.[37]

On October 9, 1998, Sharon was appointed Foreign Minister by then Prime Minister Benjamin Netanyahu. At the 1998 Wye River Peace Talks in Maryland, Sharon, serving in the capacity of Foreign Minister for Netanyahu, refused to even talk to or shake hands with Palestinian leader Yasir Arafat.[38]

In January 1999, U.S. Secretary of State Madeleine Albright refused to hold a requested meeting with Sharon in protest over Israel's refusing to enact previously signed agreements with the Palestinian Authority.

Ariel Sharon has been an outspoken opponent of the Oslo-inspired Middle East Peace Process as well as the Oslo Accords themselves.[39] Sharon argues that the current state of Jordan encompasses the true Palestinian state. This extreme view is obviously not accepted by Palestinians, Jordanians, the American Government, nor the international community.[40] Implementing the provisions of the 1993 Oslo Agreement, signed by the Israeli government of Yitzhak Rabin and the PLO, is of little importance to Sharon since he had always opposed the Oslo Peace Accords as well as the process leading up to its adoption.[41] Ariel Sharon himself wrote in 1995, "All those who sincerely mourned for Yitzhak Rabin do not obliterate for one single moment the danger the government has brought down on our heads with the Oslo Agreement. We all yearn for peace, but the Oslo agreement will not bring peace."[42]

In June 1996, Sharon wrote, "The Likud cannot accept the Oslo accords."[43] He continued, "Jerusalem will be united forever. It will be the capital of Israel only. PLO and Palestinian Authority offices will be moved out."[44]

In place of the Oslo Accords, Sharon proposed that a four-fold plan be initiated in areas handed over to the Palestinians: 1) Israel will demand the correction of all violations which must encompass an all-out war by the Palestinian Authority against terrorism; 2) The extradition of wanted murderers; 3) Confiscation of all firearms and weapons; and 4) An end to anti-Israel incitement. In territories that have not yet been handed over to the Palestinians, Sharon states, that the Likud Plan will be implemented. No more land will be turned over to the Palestinian Authorities. Sharon further argues that the Jewish settlements and other security areas must remain under exclusive Israeli control. He adds, "In addition, the main arteries connecting the coastal plain with the Jordan River and the Dead Sea will be included in the security areas, and several kilometers on each side of them."[45] To achieve a real and lasting peace with the Palestinians, Sharon needs to be more flexible with regards to territorial concessions.

On May 27, 1999, Ariel Sharon became the new leader of the Likud Party following the resignation of Benjamin Netanyahu. Sharon became even more critical of the peace process and of Barak's government after becoming Likud Party leader.

In 1999, Sharon expressed deep anger over reports that then Prime Minister Barak was trying to reach a compromise with the Palestinian Authority on the issue of Jerusalem.

Sharon declared, "Barak does not have the right to give up Jerusalem, which the people received as a legacy."[46] Keeping in mind that the issue of Jerusalem is very complicated and stirs deep emotions among all parties because of its religious significance, it must be understood that any comprehensive peace settlement between the Israelis and the Palestinians must encompass an agreement on the status of Jerusalem that is acceptable to both sides and provides for religious access to the city for all worshippers. In any case, the reality was that there was very little offered in terms of Israeli concessions regarding the status of Jerusalem under Barak.

During his campaign for Prime Minister, Sharon had proposed giving the Palestinians only half as much land as Barak had offered. This, Sharon said, would permit the Palestinians to have limited autonomy while ensuring Israel's security.[47] Sharon also criticized Barak for failing to make good on his promises on the domestic scene. According to Sharon, Barak failed to fight unemployment, improve conditions in hospitals, reform education, and narrow the socio-economic gaps among Israeli citizens.[48] Sharon wrote, "Barak is deepening animosity and internal hatred and thus endangering us all."[49] Sharon complained that Barak, in violating laws established by the Knesset, refused to report and update the head of the opposition [Likud] party on a regular basis.[50]

In criticizing Barak's government during February 2000, Sharon wrote, "One must always remember that Israel is the only place in the world where Jews have, and will always have, the right and ability to defend themselves when attacked. We cannot allow ourselves to ask others, especially American soldiers to do it for us."[51] Sharon maintained, "We all want peace, and we can achieve it with our neighbors. But it requires a different approach: negotiating without deadlines and with patience from a position of strength. Stating clear 'red lines' based on broad consensus: not leaving the Golan Heights, rejecting any attempt to divide Jerusalem; and maintaining vital security zones in Judea and Samaria in any permanent agreement."[52] By his statements, Sharon was clearly rejecting any land-for-peace solution.

In March 2000, Sharon criticized Barak strongly for negotiating with Syria and the Palestinians. Sharon attacked Barak for having lack of experience and credibility. Sharon added, "I am in favor of negotiations; I am in favor of agreements. But the government must remember that the most important thing, especially in view of the atmosphere in the Middle East, is the dimension of time. Agreements should be based on solutions that are carried out over years. Even then, we should not leave the Golan."[53] Here again, we see Sharon saying that a land-for-peace agreement is not acceptable.

In August 2000, Prime Minister Ehud Barak offered Sharon the opportunity to join his coalition government. Sharon declined the offer and responded, "Given [Barak's] numerous concessions, particularly on Jerusalem, and his failures on the domestic scene, there is no place for us in the Barak government."[54] Earlier that year, Sharon wrote, "Genuine leaders must tell the people the truth, especially in complex and difficult situations. Barak does the opposite. At best, he tells half-truths."[55] Sharon also claimed that Barak was planning to expel eighteen thousand Jews from their homes in Israeli settlements.

Editorializing in the July 21, 2000 edition of *The Jerusalem Post*, Sharon wrote, "The end to the Arab-Israeli conflict requires a clear unequivocal agreement on the termination of the state of war with all countries in the region (including Iraq, Iran, Libya, Saudi Arabia, and other peripheral states)."[56]

In the same editorial, Sharon then proposed his own six-point plan for peace in the Middle East and an end to the Arab-Israeli conflict. These included: 1) An acceptance of an undivided Jerusalem under Israeli control; 2) Israel will retain under its full control sufficiently wide security zones—in both East and West. The Jordan Valley will constitute the eastern security zone while the western security zone will encompass the line of hills commanding the coastal plain and controlling Israel's vital underground water sources. Strategic routes will be retained under Israel's control; 3) Jewish towns, villages, and communities in Judea, Samaria, and Gaza as well as all access roads will remain under full Israeli control; 4) The solution to the problem of Palestinian refugees from 1948-1967 will be based on their resettlement in the places where they live today (Jordan, Lebanon, and Syria). Israel does not accept under any circumstances the Palestinian demand for the right of return. Israel bears no moral or economic responsibility for the refugees' predicament; 5) Israel must continue to control the underground fresh water aquifers in Western Samaria, which provide a major portion of Israel's water. The Palestinians are obligated to prevent contamination of Israel's water resources; and 6) All of the territories under Palestinian control will be demilitarized. The Palestinians will not have an army; only a police force. Israel will maintain complete control of the whole air space over Judea, Samaria, and Gaza. Sharon concluded, "An agreement that terminates the conflict must include a clear and unambiguous recognition on the part of the Arab world and Arab governments, of the legitimate historical rights of the Jewish people to a Jewish state in their one and only homeland—Israel. It is necessary to arrive at a permanent and mutually obligating peace agreement that will terminate the conflict. If as a result of constraints all that we can possibly achieve is a long-term interim agreement with the Palestinians—Israel must continue to hold onto its most strategic assets."[57] Sharon added, "I believe that any government in Israel that will adopt and implement these principles will strengthen Israel's deterrence and could reach a better, more secure peace, one that will ensure Israel's long-term national strategic interests."[58]

As mentioned earlier, Sharon's September 2000 visit to the Al-Aqsa Mosque and the Temple Mount in Jerusalem sparked widespread controversy and protests by the Palestinians. Despite evidence and reports to the contrary, Sharon denied his visit to the Temple Mount was the cause of renewed Palestinian violence in the form of Intifada II. Sharon declared, "It must be clearly understood that it wasn't my visit to the Temple Mount—the holiest site for Jews under full Israeli sovereignty that ignited the current outbreak of violence."[59]

In an October 2000 letter to U.S. Secretary of State Albright, Sharon reiterated his objections to accusations that his visit to the Temple Mount ignited a new round of Palestinian protests. Sharon also remarked, "I believe we can reach peace, but it must be a durable and real peace based first and foremost on complete negation of violence. Furthermore, it requires Arab Palestinian recognition, and acceptance of certain historical inherent rights that Jews have on their land in their undivided capital of Jerusalem and particularly sovereign rights and free access to our most sacred site on the Temple Mount. This right is granted and has only been safeguarded to every Israeli citizen as well as visitors, regardless of race, creed or religion since Israel united the city in 1967."[60]

Following his election as Prime Minister, Sharon invited Ehud Barak to take over as Defense Minister and Shimon Peres to become Minister of Foreign Affairs. Peres accepted the position, however, Barak respectfully declined. Observers point out that negotiations with Arafat and Palestinian leaders will be difficult because Sharon remains inflexible on key points. Some Israeli observers maintain that it was Ehud Barak's failures that caused Sharon to be elected.[61] Sharon's platform for Prime Minister included a promise not to divide Jerusalem and to grant a much smaller portion of territory to the Palestinians than proposed by Barak. Sharon has pledged not to hand over anymore territory to the Palestinians than they currently control—forty-two percent of the West Bank and two-thirds of the Gaza Strip.[62] One can be absolutely certain that it will be impossible to achieve a real permanent peace agreement with the Palestinians without making further concessions and engaging in compromise dialogue on all of the divisive issues between Israelis and Palestinians.

Yasir Arafat and the Palestinian Authority have declared that the Israeli election, which resulted in Sharon's victory, is an "internal Israeli matter" and have called on the new Israeli government to resume talks and negotiations where they were left off under Barak.[63] In a February 11, 2001 interview, Arafat said of Sharon, "We will judge him according to the policies he takes as Prime Minister and with whom he will form a government."[64]

As Prime Minister, Sharon has repeatedly maintained that he will not meet with or hold direct negotiations with Arafat or Palestinian Authorities until the Palestinians end their uprising against Israel. Sharon claims that Arafat has failed to end the violence and arresting Palestinian militants who are engaging in attacks on Israel. On another occasion, Sharon added, "Arafat is our bin Laden."[65] Despite the shortcomings of Arafat and the Palestinian Authority, statements like these may be counterproductive to the peace process.

Sharon has stated repeatedly that there would "not be negotiations under fire."[66] He has further maintained, "Before entry into negotiations, there will be a total cease-fire. Only that way it is possible to reach peace."[67] Sharon is right in demanding a cease-fire, however, he too must be willing to make concessions. Sharon needs to halt Israeli settlements in Palestinian areas and end his government's policy of home demolitions and targeted assassinations if he sincerely wants peace. Once these have been accomplished, the Palestinian Authority can be held fully accountable in controlling militants and enforcing cease-fire provisions in areas under its control.

During his first three months as Prime Minister, Sharon sent his oldest son, Omri, as an envoy to Palestinian Authority Leader Yasir Arafat. Sharon has refused to meet with Palestinian Authorities directly "until there is an end to the violence."[68] Sharon denied Palestinian and Labor Party claims that he was placing a roadblock in the way of peace. He argued that by sending his son as an envoy, he was keeping with the Arab tribal culture to send one's own flesh and blood as a sign of respect. Sharon and Omri live together in a ranch in Israel's Negev Desert.[69]

In July 2001, Sharon told *Newsweek* reporter Larry Weymouth, "Oslo didn't bring peace. It didn't bring security."[70] Sharon further stated, "The people responsible for that terrible mistake, the Oslo Agreement, would like to justify what they have done."[71] In the same interview, Sharon also commented, "I am ready to make painful compromises for a true peace. But I will not make any compromises that endanger the security of the Israeli people."[72] In a January 2001 issue of *Kfar Habad*, an orthodox Jewish weekly, Sharon discussed what he meant by painful compromises. Sharon stated, "When I talk about painful concessions, I mean that we will not reoccupy Nablus and Jericho and other places. For me, this is a very painful concession."[73]

Sharon argues that Arafat is an obstacle to true peace. When asked if he could reach a lasting settlement with Arafat, Sharon stated, "I don't think you can make a deal with a terrorist organization."[74] Again, Sharon is right in insisting that the violence stop and in demanding security guarantees for Israel, however, Sharon too must also be willing to make real concessions. Sharon cannot have it both ways. He cannot target for attack Palestinian police posts, disarm Palestinian police officers, refuse to meet with Arafat, instigate tensions with Palestinians by increasing Israeli settlements, demolish the homes of Palestinian families, and disregard the Oslo Peace Accords as a basis for future agreements while expecting Arafat and the Palestinian Authority to control militants. Even though Arafat leaves much to be desired, he and the Palestinian Authority need additional autonomy as well as cooperation and commitment from Sharon and the Israeli government to establish a permanent peace agreement on the basis of the Oslo Peace Accords, which Netanyahu and Barak both worked to undermine. The reason why extremist Palestinian militants and opposition groups like Hamas and Islamic Jihad are gaining support and popularity is because many Palestinians are growing impatient with the constant change of attitude and approach toward peace within the Israeli government. Many other Palestinians are turning against the Palestinian Authority because they have been unable to deliver a final and permanent peace settlement resulting in an independent Palestinian state and rooted in the Oslo Accords.

Israel has doubled the number of Jewish settlers in the West Bank and Gaza from one hundred thousand to two hundred thousand since the signing of the Oslo Peace Accords in 1993. Since taking office in February, Sharon, despite pressure and requests from the United States government to halt settlement activities, has been still rapidly expanding Israeli settlements in and around Palestinian communities.[75] These settlement expansions serve only to aggravate an already delicate situation and greatly injure prospects for peace between Israelis and Palestinians.

Will Prime Minister Ariel Sharon be able to stop the violence, guarantee security, and bring about a lasting peace for the state of Israel? After looking at his record objectively, one cannot help but be pessimistic. In writing of Sharon, *BBC News* Correspondent Tarik Kafal observed, "If his record is anything to go by, he will make no concessions to the Palestinians on Jerusalem, keep all the settlements under Israeli sovereignty, and come down hard on the Palestinian uprising using the full force of the Israeli army."[76] This kind of hard-line approach will render any meaningful peace agreement virtually impossible.

4

Post-Oslo: The Mitchell Report &
The U.S. Role As Mediator

Former President Bill Clinton created a fact-finding commission following the October 2000 Middle East Peace talks held in Sharm-el-Sheikh, Egypt. The role of the Commission was to find out what factors contributed to the renewed violence that followed the failed Peace Talks between Arafat and Barak at Camp David and to explore ways to achieve a permanent settlement between the Israelis and Palestinians. The Commission was chaired by former U.S. Senator George Mitchell (D-Maine) and included former U.S. Senator Warren Rudman (R-NH). The Commission's findings were released and made public in May 2001. What has become known as the 'Mitchell Report' concluded, "Fear, hate, anger, and frustration have risen on both sides. The greatest danger of all is that the culture of peace, nurtured over the past decade, is being shattered."[1]

The Report continued, "Two proud people share a land and a destiny. Their competing claims and religious differences have led to a grinding, demoralizing, dehumiliating conflict. They can continue in conflict, or they can negotiate to find a way to live side-by-side in peace."[2] The Mitchell Report explained, "We complied with the request that we would not determine guilt or innocence."[3] The Commission, when established by President Clinton, had been told not to place blame on either party for the escalated violence.

The Mitchell Report stated that "terrorism is reprehensible and unacceptable" and called on the Palestinian Authority to take "immediate steps to apprehend and incarcerate terrorists operating within the PA's [Palestinian Authority's] jurisdiction."[4]

The Mitchell Report findings stated that the process that began during the signing of the Oslo Peace Accords has come under intense scrutiny by both the Israeli and Palestinian peoples. It stated, "Both sides see the lack of full compliance with agreements reached since the opening of the peace process as evidence of a lack of good faith. This conclusion led to an erosion of trust even before the permanent-status negotiations began."[5]

The recommendations made by the Mitchell Report were three-fold: 1) End the violence; 2) Rebuild Confidence; and 3) Resume negotiations. In discussing the first recommendation on ending the violence, the Report states that the Israeli government and Palestinian Authority should both act swiftly to stop the violence and reaffirm the commitment to existing agreements in order to begin a series of new negotiations. In considering the second step of rebuilding confidence, the Report recommends a 'cooling-off period' and the implementation of confidence-building measures. This means that both Palestinians and Israelis must acknowledge that acts of violence are unacceptable. In discussing the third step of resuming negotiations, the Report recommends that future negotiations must "manifest a spirit of compromise, reconciliation and partnership, not withstanding the events of the past seven months."[6]

According to the Report, the Palestinian Authority must: 1) Renew cooperation with Israel in order to ensure security guarantees; and 2) Prevent Palestinian gunmen from using Palestinian populated areas to fire upon Israeli populated areas. The Israeli government must: 1) Freeze all settlement activity, including the 'natural growth' of existing settlements; 2) Withdraw military forces to positions held before September 28, 2000, which will reduce the number of violent confrontations; 3) Encourage non-lethal responses to unarmed Palestinian protestors; and 4) Lift closures, transfer all tax revenues owed, and permit Palestinians who work in Israel to return to their jobs.[7]

The Report also acknowledged the political difficulties facing both Israelis and Palestinians. It concluded, "Israelis do not wish to be perceived as 'rewarding violence.' Palestinians do not wish to be received as 'rewarding occupation.' We appreciate the political constraints of the leaders of both sides. Nevertheless, if the cycle of violence is to be broken and the search for peace resumed, there needs to be a new bilateral relationship incorporating both security cooperation and negotiations."[8]

United Nations Secretary-General Kofi Annan expressed optimism about the Mitchell Report findings. Annan stated, "I think there are elements in it which should allow the parties to step back and take steps for a cease-fire, confidence-building measures, and eventually, return to the table."[9]

Palestinian Authority leader Yasir Arafat welcomed the Mitchell Report and called for a summit to be held in order to implement its provisions.[10] In reacting to the Mitchell Report, the Palestinian Authority stated, "The findings and recommendations of the report offer Palestinians and Israelis a sensible and coherent foundation for resolving the current crisis and preparing the path for resuming meaningful negotiations."[11] The Israeli government responded to the Mitchell Report by demanding that the Palestinians cease all violent actions and uprisings before talks can be convened. On May 21, 2001, in responding to the Mitchell Report, Israeli Prime Minister Sharon commented, "The Mitchell Report is acceptable to us in principle. We had comments, which we conveyed; and they were clear."[12] Based upon the information presented here, one can presume that Sharon's conveyed comments probably pertained to his opposition to freezing Israeli settlement expansions in Palestinian territories. Sharon, like Barak before him, has consistently supported the expansion of Israeli settlements in Palestinian areas. The settlement issue remains a sticking point in negotiations between the Israeli government and Palestinians.

U.S. Secretary of State Colin Powell commented, "So both sides have commissioned this report, have accepted this report, and it's now time for both sides, with the help of the international community and the United States, to move forward on the basis of this report."[13]

Following publication of the Report, Senator George Mitchell told *Reuters News Agency*, "The United States is a very strong supporter and ally of Israel. But even in such close relationships there are differences of opinion. Every American administration for the past 25 years has opposed the actions and policies of the government of Israel with respect to settlements."[14]

Since Israel has already signed peace agreements with Egypt and Jordan, Syria and Lebanon remain the current bordering nations without an agreement. The dispute between Syria and Israel involves the status of the Golan Heights and access to the Sea of Galilee. The situation in Lebanon is far more complex since that country is still dealing with the consequences of a tragic civil war that lasted from early 1975 to the early 1990's. The weakened Lebanese government has been unable to control Palestinian militants, including Hamas and the Islamic Jihad, operating out of southern Lebanon, from attacking Israel or preventing border skirmishes between Israelis and Palestinians. A peace treaty signed by Israel and Jordan allowed for Jordanian control of Muslim holy sights in Jerusalem. Since the government of Jordan has renounced all claims to the West Bank, negotiations and a permanent agreement between the Israeli government and the Palestinian Authority, as well as an agreement with Syria regarding the Golan Heights, remain most crucial to bringing about stability in the region.

A permanent settlement between the Israelis and Palestinian Authority depends upon the a resolution of the following important and complex issues between the parties:

1. **The status of Israeli settlements in the West Bank and Gaza Strip**

2. **The return of Palestinian refugees**

3. **Security guarantees for Israel**

4. **The creation of an independent Palestinian state with its own police force consistent with United Nations Resolution 181 and 242**

5. **An agreement on the status of Jerusalem that permits access to all worshippers**

As mentioned earlier, United Nations Resolution 181 proposes that the City of Jerusalem be internationalized. This position has also been adopted by the Catholic Church and the Vatican. United Nations Resolution 242 calls upon Israel to withdraw to its 1967 borders and allow for the establishment of an independent Palestinian state in the Gaza Strip and West Bank. The status of Jerusalem will be a major point of contention between both parties. As discussed earlier, Prime Minister Ariel Sharon has declared on a number of occasions that a united Jerusalem will remain under Israeli jurisdiction and control. The issue of Jerusalem is so divisive because of the religious significance and holy sites that this great City contains. Jerusalem has long been a point of contention and battleground for the world's great religions, Judaism, Christianity, and Islam, for over two thousand years. The Israelis want to keep a united Jerusalem as their capital while the Palestinians want to have a portion of Jerusalem as their capital of an independent Palestine. The present-day Gaza Strip encompasses about three hundred and seventy square miles and approximately nine hundred and fifty thousand people. As of 1998, there were about six thousand Israeli settlers living in Gaza Strip developments. Israel had actually originally promised autonomy to the Gaza Strip region during the 1978 Camp David Accords when it signed a peace treaty with Egypt.[15]

Currently, the number of Palestinian refugees and their descendents in the Israeli-occupied territories totals over three million people.[16] In an interview with *Newsweek* in March 2001, Prime Minister-Elect Ariel Sharon expressed optimism about his ability to achieve lasting peace with the Palestinians. Sharon stated, "I believe I can make peace because I saw all the horrors of wars. I participated in all the wars and lost my best friends in battles. I was seriously injured twice. Therefore, I understand the importance of peace better than the politicians who speak about peace but never experienced war."[17] One can only hope that Sharon is sincere in these statements however, his actions and other writings paint a different picture. Sharon's past actions indicate that he wants peace only if it can be achieved on his own terms. If his present terms resemble his past proposals, peace will not be achieved and more innocent Palestinian and Israeli lives will be lost.

Since the new government of Ariel Sharon has stated that the concessions made by the Barak government are off the table, Sharon is expected to propose a more modest deal, trading a small amount of land or economic benefits for Palestinian non-belligerency. Raanan Gisson, Sharon's spokesman, has declared, "Everything in Camp David is null and void unless it was signed, and nothing was signed."[18] In January 2001, while campaigning for Prime Minister, Sharon himself stated, "The Oslo Agreement is finished. It doesn't exist."[19] A lasting peace settlement between the Israeli government and the Palestinian Authority will require recognition of the Oslo Peace Accords as a basis for future negotiations.

Frustration and tensions have been rising on the Palestinian side. In the spring of 2001, the Fatah, Arafat's political movement within the PLO, had threatened to intensify the Intifada within the territories. In a public statement, Fatah leaders warned, "If Israelis think that Sharon will make security for them, we say loudly that Israel will have no security at all."[20] Both the Palestinians and Israelis have employed terrorist tactics to achieve their goals. Palestinian militants have attacked Israeli civilians and engaged in suicide missions while Israel has employed methods of terrorism in attempting to crush the Palestinian struggle for self-determination and by using methods of torture to extract information. All of these need to stop.

The Israeli government charges that the Palestinian Authorities, including Arafat himself, are operating in direct violation of their promises. They point to statements by Palestinian Authorities, including Arafat himself. In 1997, for example, Arafat declared, "The [Israeli] settlements are a declaration of total war against the Palestinian people."[21] A similar comment was made by Farrouk Kaddumi, the head of PLO's Fatah. Kaddumi stated, "The only option in this situation is to continue the Uprising since this is the only language that Israel understands." [22] Peaceful demonstrations by Palestinians to protest deplorable living conditions and to demand autonomy are a recognized form of free expression, however, when these demonstrations result in armed conflict against innocent Israeli civilians, this is a serious and an unacceptable obstacle to peace.

Some Palestinian observers assert that Arafat is being forced to bargain from an unfair strength: the use of terrorism. They point to the expansion of Israeli settlements in Palestinian areas, the treatment of Palestinian citizens by Israeli authorities, and the sporadic changes in Israeli government leaders that results in changes in approaches and strategies for reaching a final peace settlement based upon the Oslo Accords. The Israeli government, under Sharon, is criticizing Arafat for not being forceful enough in controlling Palestinian militants and extremists while at the same time, holding Arafat in confinement and withholding revenues owed to the Palestinian Authority. Arafat is also facing heavy criticism from the radical Hamas, an Islamic Palestinian fundamentalist group that opposes the peace process and the Oslo Accords. Hamas leader Ibrahim Yazaroorie complains that Palestinian leaders and the PLO have "compromised too much" with Israel.[23] Even so, Arafat and the Palestinian Authority leaders must take a more proactive role in condemning hostile propaganda statements directed against Israel by Palestinian radio and newspapers since the spring of 2000. These actions clearly violate the spirit of the Oslo Peace Accords and serve only to disrupt the peace process.

In 2001, *The Boston Globe* editorialized, "Arafat is now under threat from Sharon on one side and Hamas on the other. The Israelis and Palestinians who believe they will be better off without him may find, however, that the alternatives are far worse."[24] The *Globe* editorial continued, "If [President] Bush does not endorse American mediation that pressures the two sides to draw back from a point of no return, Arafat may be swept aside and Sharon and Hamas will be left to carry on a violent dialogue between Israelis and Palestinians."[25] In addition, the *Globe* pointed out, "The danger is plain. Sharon has not tried to hide the fact that he is following a policy of restraint because it has succeeded in temporarily altering international opinion in Israel's favor."[26] In other words, Sharon is working overtime to win world sympathy and to convert the majority of the Israeli public to his agenda of opposing the Oslo Peace Accords, the implementation of its provisions, the creation of an independent Palestinian state, and the finalization of a lasting peace settlement with the Palestinian Authority.

Professor Jeff Halper, Coordinator of the Israeli Committee Against House Demolitions, maintains that Sharon's 'national unity' government represents a refusal of Israel to entertain the possibility of truly sharing this land with the Palestinians—either in one state or in two.[27] According to Professor Halper, Sharon's 'national unity' government has no political program other than to engineer the surrender of the Palestinians."[28] In order to accomplish this goal, Sharon knows that he must win over public opinion and world sympathy.

Newsweek correspondent Joshua Hammer has reported that new Israeli checkpoints and blockades have been established in the West Bank with the goal of halting communication between Palestinian leaders. Hammer writes, "The Israeli government insists that a blockade of the West Bank is helping contain the violence, but it may be doing exactly the opposite: intensifying Palestinians' economic misery and rage, while failing for the most part to prevent a determined terrorist from sneaking into the country." [29] In response to violent protests and attacks by Palestinians, the Israeli government has engaged in a policy of increasing Israeli settlements in Palestinian areas and demolishing the homes of Palestinian civilians and families.[30]

The Israeli government, under Sharon, further maintains that the United States should remove itself from taking an active role in the peace process because the Palestinians have shown that they really do not desire peace.[31] According to the *Associated Press*, President George W. Bush's administration has indicated that it will not mediate as heavily as the previous administration of former President Bill Clinton. Instead, President Bush has called on Israelis and Palestinians to take the lead in negotiating a settlement themselves.[32] All of this raises an important ethical question, "Does the United States have a moral obligation to help mediate the Middle East Peace Process?"

According to the Israeli press, U.S. Secretary of State Colin Powell has told Israeli leaders that the United States has returned to strongly advancing its traditional policy of considering the expansion of Israeli settlements in occupied Palestinian territories to be illegal and an obstacle to peace. This long-time American stance had been relaxed during the Clinton administration.[33]

Angry Palestinians maintain that American financial assistance to Israel has resulted in American tax dollars paying for bombs and weaponry that Israel uses against Palestinians. Palestinian leaders argue that Israel's dependence on American financial, moral, and political support puts the United States in an ideal position to help facilitate a permanent agreement. The Palestinian Authority also claims that the Clinton administration previously established a role for the United States Government as the mediator and that the United States should assume responsibility and live up to its previous commitments and obligations.[34] Mahmoud Abbas, then a senior Palestinian leader in the West Bank and now Prime Minister of the Palestinian Authority, has stated, "The American role is not enough and not acceptable. We need American intervention now."[35]

The Israeli government under Sharon is asking that the United States continue to assist Israel financially and politically while maintaining a hands-off approach to the peace process. The current Israeli government and its supporters argue that negotiations between the Israeli government and the Palestinians encompass an internal matter that should be resolved by the parties themselves since the United States is not directly affected by the process itself. Sharon wants the United States to remove itself from the negotiations and take a backseat role in the Middle East peace process.[36]

Regarding the ethical question of "Does the United States have a moral obligation to help mediate the Middle East peace process," I would answer Yes. The international community and the United Nations have recognized the existence of the Palestinian Authority and have called for the creation of an independent Palestinian state to coexist alongside the state of Israel. The most important justification for my reasoning is that the United States already assumed responsibility for facilitating this role. In foreign affairs, it is important that we live up to and keep our commitments. Besides, it was the mediation efforts of the United States that led to the signing of the Oslo Peace Accords in the first place.

In addition to the issue of Jerusalem, the Palestinians complain that peace negotiations have dragged on for seven years without a final agreement and that because of this they reject the new long-term interim agreements proposed by Israel.[37] Palestinian Authority Leader Yasir Arafat has consistently demanded an end to Israeli settlement expansions in Palestinian territories. The United States government and the world community have publicly acknowledged that the continuing expansion of Israeli settlements in Palestinian territories constitutes a major obstacle to reaching a final peace agreement between the Israeli government and the Palestinian Authority.

CIA Director George Tenet arranged a cease-fire between Israel and the Palestinians on June 12, 2001. The so-called Tenet Plan required Israel to pull back its military troops from Palestinian areas to be relocated to positions they held in September 2000. The Tenet Plan also required the Palestinian Authority to enforce the cease-fire, resume security cooperation with the Israeli government, arrest Palestinian militants from the extremist groups Hamas and Islamic Jihad, and to collect illegal weapons. Although Arafat accepted this proposal, many other Palestinian leaders voiced strong opposition to it and demanded that the full Mitchell Report be incorporated into any cease-fire arrangement.[38]

The Israeli government also complained that Arafat has been unable or unwilling to control Palestinian militants from attacking Israel since the cease-fire was arranged. This is true but by closing Palestinian police posts, holding tax revenues, and refusing to provide adequate resources to the Palestinian Authority, the Sharon government has complicated the tensions and made it all the more difficult for the Palestinian Authority and Arafat to control the militants. Militant Palestinian groups, who oppose peace with Israel, are gaining support and popularity among Palestinians because of the current state of affairs. Again, Arafat still has a responsibility to speak out against and strongly condemn Palestinian militants utilizing terrorism against innocent civilians as a retaliatory measure but, Sharon too must accept his share of responsibility for escalating tensions.

Palestinian security officers claim that their authority to halt attacks against Israel are limited. Jibril Rajoub, the Palestinian Authority's West Bank Security Chief claims that only eighteen percent of the West Bank is under his jurisdiction and he can only control these areas. Rajoub further maintains that Arafat has control only over the areas under his jurisdiction.

When questioned as to if the Palestinian Authority has started to re-arrest people who have committed acts of terrorism against Israel, Rajoub responded, "If the Israelis arrest the settlers and soldiers who have killed innocent Palestinians during the last six months, I think it is fair to ask the Palestinians to do the same."[39] This again illustrates the difficulty and complexity of the problem of achieving cooperation on both sides.

The Palestinian Authority has repeatedly requested third party intervention to observe and help resolve the dispute between Israelis and Palestinians. Arafat has called for an international peacekeeping force to observe the West Bank and Gaza Strip.[40] This request has been refused by the Israeli governments of Netanyahu, Barak, and Sharon.

In March 2001, the United Nations proposed a resolution backing an observer force for the Palestinians. The resolution called upon United Nations Secretary-General Kofi Annan to work with both parties "on setting up a protection mechanism to contribute to the protection of Palestinian civilians." Exercising its veto power for the first time since 1997, the United States killed the resolution.[41] A voluntary international peacekeeping force would be beneficial since it could objectively monitor the situation in the region while peace negotiations are taking place.

Despite demands from the United States to halt Israeli settlements in Palestinian areas, Sharon has vowed to continue expanding these settlements. Sharon has declared, "We will build. Homes will be built in accordance with our current needs."[42] Sharon's government has already allocated three hundred and sixty million dollars for the construction of new homes and Jewish settlements in order to accommodate what the Israeli government refers to as 'natural growth' of existing communities.[43]

The United States has called the Israeli policies and practices of home demolition "provocative." State Department Spokesman Richard Boucher has called on Israel to stop demolishing the homes of Palestinian civilians. Boucher stated,

"Actions such as these are provocative and undermine relations between the parties and can only make more difficult efforts to restore calm."[44]

Pope John Paul II and the Vatican have called upon Sharon and the Israeli government to withdraw from Palestinian territories, accept U.N. Resolutions, abide by the principles of the Geneva Convention, and recognize the right of the Palestinians to self-determination.[45]

Since his defeat for re-election as Prime Minister, Ehud Barak has been blaming Arafat and the Palestinian Authorities for the failure of the parties to reach an agreement. The truth is Barak is trying to cover for his own shortcomings and failures by blaming others. The fact that the Israeli election in February 2001 resulted in the lowest voter-turnout in Israel's history speaks for itself about the quality of the candidates, namely Barak and Sharon.

In June 2001, the *Associated Press* reported that Prime Minister Ariel Sharon was clashing with his Foreign Minister Shimon Peres by refusing to permit a meeting between the Israeli government and Arafat.[46] In November 2002, Peres resigned his position in the Sharon government over a disagreement on Israeli settlements in the Occupied territories triggering a call for new elections. This will be discussed further in detail later on.

The Israeli government has also been following a policy of targeting Palestinian police posts for shelling. This obviously further weakens the ability of the Palestinian Authority leaders who want peace, to control the militants and terrorists.

Conservative factions in Israel have been calling for a full-scale military invasion of Palestinian territories in the West Bank and Gaza Strip in order to suppress the Palestinian uprising. There have been reports that Sharon's government has been considering an all-out military invasion of areas under Palestinian control. Raanan Gisson, Sharon's spokesman, commented, "There are three options: surrender to Arafat, to go ahead with this plan—to occupy—or to continue the current course of restraint and self-defense. The government has said it's committed to peace but this situation can't last forever."[47]

The only way to achieve a lasting peace between Israelis and Palestinians is for both parties to acknowledge and guarantee security for Israel as well as the right of Palestinians to self-determination and statehood in the West Bank and Gaza Strip, access to East Jerusalem, and the Right of Return of displaced Palestinian refugees. These were the driving principles rooted in the provisions of the Oslo Peace Accords.

5

Palestinian Authority Reforms &
The Quartet Plan

Since the Intifada was instituted again in September 2000, over three thousand people have been killed, including at least two thousand five hundred Palestinians and five hundred Israelis as of June 2003.

When looking at the current state of affairs, there are five possible outcomes to the Israeli-Palestinian conflict: 1) Status quo with Israel retaining control of the occupied territories; 2) Unification of Israelis and Palestinians into a single secular nation; 3) Partition into two states, one Jewish, and one Palestinian; 4) Expulsion of Palestinians; and 5) Elimination of Israel.[1] Most observers would probably agree that the first outcome of status quo is likely to prevail since Israel remains very capable of defeating both the Palestinians and the surrounding Arab countries.

Peace did occur with the signing of the Oslo Peace Accords from the fall of 1993 to September 2000. Although there were isolated incidents of aggression on both sides, Israelis and Palestinians for the most part, did live in peace and security without an organized Intifada Uprising. This peace was largely the result of Palestinians witnessing an end to what they viewed as the oppression of Israeli occupiers and the beginning of Palestinian self-rule in the West Bank and Gaza Strip. The failure of both sides to reach a permanent peace agreement rooted in the Oslo Accords helped to ignite another round of Palestinian Uprisings in September 2000.

Up until this point, a great deal of discussion in this work has centered around Israeli government policies and the Israeli leadership. The reason for this is that since 1988 not one Israeli government has served a full four-year term. As a result, Israeli government policies have changed continuously to reflect each of the new government regimes culminating with the election of Ariel Sharon as Prime Minister who pledged to undo the Oslo Peace Accords. The Palestinian

Authority, on the other hand, has remained relatively the same under the leadership of Yasir Arafat since his first election as President in 1996. Arafat's leadership too has left much to be desired. He has ruled more like a dictator than as a democratically-elected President. He has also excluded certain minority political parties from involvement in his government and has worked to suppress all opposition to his policies. There is no question that the Palestinian Authority under the leadership of Yasir Arafat has been plagued by corruption and scandal. Under Arafat's leadership, the Palestinian economy has declined greatly, the Gross Domestic Product [GDP] has fallen by seventy percent, the public infrastructure has collapsed, and public health standards have fallen dramatically. This is despite the fact that the Palestinian Authority has received billions of dollars in financial assistance from the international community, including the United States. In 1997, the Palestinian Authority received more than one billion dollars in international assistance and Palestinian tax revenues. By the end of the year, three hundred and twenty three million dollars was unaccounted for in the Palestinian Authority's annual report. Another example of Palestinian Authority mismanagement is of twenty million dollars that had been given to the Palestinian Mortgage Housing Corporation by the European Union for the purpose of building low-cost housing in the Gaza Strip for the Palestinian population. The European Union later discovered that the funds had been used to build luxury housing for supporters of Yasir Arafat. It was also documented that Arafat deposited over five million dollars in Arab nation assistance to the Palestinian Authority into his personal account.[2]

These activities and mismanagement on the part of the Palestinian Authority have also stifled the peace process by creating a loss of confidence on the part of many Israelis, Palestinians, and members of the international community in the ability of the Palestinian Authority to properly manage resources on behalf of the Palestinian people. It could also be argued that these failures by the Palestinian Authority have contributed to the creation and popularity of Palestinian resistance movements opposing the peace process and engaging in terrorist attacks against the Israeli people.

In June 2002, Israeli troops re-occupied much of the West Bank areas that had previously been under the control of the Palestinian Authority. The Israeli government argued that this was a necessary response in the wake of a series of Palestinian suicide bombings against Israel. The Palestinian Authority, as could be expected, condemned what they viewed as a harsh Israeli response of collective punishment and countered that the only way to quell the terrorist activities of Palestinian militants was to remove illegal Israeli settlements in the West Bank and Gaza Strip and to continue forward with a peace process that would lead to a permanent and comprehensive settlement.

The Israeli government also responded to Palestinian terror attacks by demolishing homes of suspected militants and their families, engaging in targeted killings of Palestinian militant leaders, and building new Israeli settlements in predominately Palestinian areas of the West Bank and Gaza Strip. The end result of these Palestinian terror attacks and the Israeli responses has been increased tensions between Israelis and Palestinians and a further straining of peace efforts.

The Palestinian Authority has repeatedly condemned the terrorist attacks and suicide bombings directed at Israel, however, Palestinian leaders have argued that the Israeli response of targeted killings, new settlements, and home demolitions have only escalated the situation and made problems worse. During the fall 2002, the British government, signaling agreement with the Palestinian Authority's position, led by Prime Minister Tony Blair, imposed an embargo on the export of defense equipment to Israel in order to respond to and express disapproval of Sharon's aggressive military response in re-occupying Palestinian areas and directing collective punishment of the Palestinian population.

In January 2003, the Labor Party bolted from Sharon's coalition government claiming that Sharon was not serious about making peace and reaching a comprehensive settlement with the Palestinians. This caused the Israeli government to be dissolved and forced new elections once again. Sharon's opponent for Prime Minister was Amram Mitzna, the Mayor of Haifa and leader of the opposition Labor Party. Mitzna campaigned in favor of a land-for-peace statehood settlement with the Palestinians and for re-opening full discussion and negotiations with Palestinian Authority President Arafat. On January 28, 2003, Ariel Sharon won a sweeping campaign for re-election and nearly doubled his Likud Party's parliamentary strength from nineteen to thirty-seven seats within the one hundred twenty-member parliament. The Labor Party representation, on the other hand, dropped from twenty-six to nineteen parliamentary seats.[3]

Following Ariel Sharon's re-election bid, his Likud Party website stated that the Israeli Prime Minister and Likud Party leaders are determined to apply the principles established by Sharon in founding the Likud Party in 1973, including a hard-line approach in dealing with the Palestinians.

In January 2003, Arafat called on Sharon to return to the negotiating table and to meet with him to discuss specifics as soon as possible. Sharon responded to these calls by blaming Arafat for inciting violence against Israel and not doing enough to suppress terrorism. Sharon has also called on the Palestinian people to replace Arafat with a more formidable partner for peace.

Sharon had asked his former rival Mitzna and the Labor Party to join his new coalition government, however, they turned down the offer insisting that Sharon was not serious about achieving a comprehensive land-for-peace settlement with the Palestinians. The Labor Party demanded that Sharon first dismantle some Israeli settlements in the West Bank and Gaza and immediately resume talks with the Palestinian leaders. Mitzna stated, "We will remind Sharon every day that there is an alternative, that there is another way."[4] As a result of Labor's refusal to join, Sharon formed a right-wing partnership government between the Likud and the far-right National Union and National Religious Party in conjunction with the centrist Shinui Party.

In response to U.S.-led peace initiatives, Sharon has stated that if the violence stops he could envision a limited Palestinian state in land currently under the jurisdiction of the Palestinian Authority. This vision falls short of what the Palestinian Authority is calling for and has even drawn criticism from the United States. U.S. Secretary of State Colin Powell has responded that the Palestinian state would have to be a "real state, not a phony state that is diced into a thousand different pieces."[5]

During the fall of 2002, President George W. Bush instructed his foreign policy advisors to draft a blueprint plan for peace in the Middle East between the Arab nations and Israel and a permanent settlement of the Israeli-Palestinian conflict. This plan was drafted by the United States with input from Russia, the European Union, and the United Nations. In its early stages this plan was referred to as the Quartet Peace Plan because it was written by the aforementioned four parties. The plan serves as a great outline of the terms and conditions necessary for all sides to agree to if a permanent settlement is to be achieved.

On April 30, 2003, shortly after the U.S.-led War on Iraq, the U.S. State Department released the official copy of what has become known as the "Road Map To Peace" between the Israelis and the Palestinians. This plan was consistent with and reaffirmed the contents of the Mitchell Report. This document encompasses the specifics of the Quartet Plan. The Road Map outlines three steps or phases that the Palestinian Authority and the Israeli government must each take to reach a permanent settlement. The Road Map also includes a tentative timeline for implementing its provisions. The end goal of the Road Map is a permanent peace settlement between the parties that results in the acceptance of a two-state solution (Palestine and Israel living side by side) between the Israelis and Palestinians by 2005.

The Road Map also calls on the leaders of the Arab world to normalize diplomatic and trade relations with Israel prior to the completion of the Road Map. A meeting of the Arab League in Beirut, Lebanon during the spring of 2002 resulted in unanimous endorsement by the Arab countries of a Saudi Arabian proposal by Crown Prince Abdullah for Arab acceptance of Israel as a neighbor living in peace and security in the context of a comprehensive peace settlement. This was obviously a very positive and historic development paving the way for future talks and peace settlements.

As mentioned earlier, the Quartet Plan Road Map To Peace included three phases. Phase 1, which is scheduled to occur by the end of May 2003, calls on the Palestinians to take all measures necessary to achieve an unconditional cessation of violence and terrorism against Israel and to undertake comprehensive political reform in preparation for statehood, including drafting a Palestinian Constitution that encompasses a parliamentary democratic system and to hold free, fair, and open elections for their government leaders. These reforms of the Palestinian Authority are necessary for the reasons cited earlier, namely to end the corruption and restore public confidence in the ability of the Palestinian Authority to manage its own affairs and to be a willing and trusting partner in the peace process. The Palestinian Authority is also required to issue an "unequivocal" statement reiterating Israel's right to exist in peace and security and to crack down on militants encouraging incitement of violence and terror against Israel. Israel, likewise, is called upon to take steps to normalize Palestinian life, to withdraw from areas occupied after September 28, 2000, to halt its home demolitions policy and attacks on Palestinian civilians as collective punishment, to refrain from engaging in the destruction of Palestinian infrastructure and institutions, and to affirm its commitment to the two-state vision of an independent and sovereign Palestinian state living in peace and security alongside Israel, as expressed by President Bush. This phase also calls upon the Arab countries to end their financial and moral support to organizations supporting and engaging in violence and terror against Israel.

Phase II of the Road Map involves the creation of an independent Palestinian state with provisional borders and attributes of sovereignty by December 2003 after the Palestinian leadership has acted decisively against terror. The progress of Phase II will be based upon the consensus judgment of the Quartet (United States, Russia, United Nations, and European Union) on whether the conditions are appropriate to proceed. Phase II also encompasses the normalization of relations between Israel and her Arab neighbors. This will include cooperation on issues of trade, security, arms control, sharing of resources, economic development, and refugees. Finally, Phase II will also provide for an international role, monitored by the Quartet members, in overseeing the transition.

Phase III involves a permanent status agreement and end of the Israeli-Palestinian conflict in 2004-2005. Like Phase II, progress into Phase III is based on a consensus judgment of the Quartet parties. The beginning of this phase involves an agreement on the status of an independent Palestinian state with provisional borders in 2004 which will lead to a final, permanent status resolution in 2005 on borders, Jerusalem, refugees, settlements, and progress toward a comprehensive Middle East peace settlement between Israel and Lebanon and Israel and Syria, to be achieved as soon as possible. Phase III also requires Arab state acceptance of full normal relations with Israel and security for all the nations of the region in the context of a comprehensive Arab-Israeli peace.

The reaction by Palestinians and Israelis to the Quartet Plan Road Map To Peace has been mixed. The Palestinian Authority has fully accepted the Quartet Road Map and has started to implement its provisions. This has included the appointment of Mahmoud Abbas, also known as Abu Mazen, as Prime Minister of the Palestinian Authority as part of an internal reform and reorganization plan for the Palestinian Authority demanded by Israel and the United States as a condition for re-opening negotiations between the Israeli government and Palestinian leaders. This was viewed as a preliminary step forward since the Israeli government, under Prime Minister Ariel Sharon, has refused to meet and negotiate with Palestinian Authority President Arafat for reasons cited earlier. Abbas is a highly-respected and well-educated leader in the Palestinian Authority. He is admired by many Palestinians and Israelis alike. Abbas is viewed as a moderate and is credited with being the chief architect behind the 1993 Oslo Peace Accords. The Palestinian Parliament confirmed Abbas's appointment as Prime Minister on April 29, 2003. Abbas has promised to take all steps necessary to end the Intifada and terror attacks against Israel. This is hopeful news. Even so, it must be noted that even though Abbas will now be the chief negotiator for the Palestinians, any agreement that he negotiates must, by Palestinian Authority law, also be approved by Arafat. Abbas also personally endorsed the Quartet Plan Road Map To Peace in May 2003. Now the biggest challenge facing Abbas will be to make good on his promise to end the violence and incitement against Israel and to then secure positive confidence-building measures from the Sharon government, including the halting of Israeli settlements.

The Israeli government response to the Bush-baked Quartet Plan Road Map To Peace has been even more sporadic. In January 2003, when asked to comment on the early stages of the plan, Ariel Sharon responded, "Oh, the Quartet is nothing. Don't take it seriously."[6] Since that time, the Bush Administration has been putting tremendous pressure on Sharon and Israeli government leaders to accept the plan. Some progress was made on May 26, 2003 when the Israeli government approved the Quartet Plan Road Map To Peace with major conditions attached. The Israeli government approved the "steps defined by the road map" but not the entire document.[7] One of the major reservations by Israel included the right of return of up to four million Palestinian refugees to the West Bank and Gaza Strip in a newly created Palestinian state. This right of return of Palestinian refugees is scheduled to be negotiated in the third and final stage of the Quartet Peace Plan. On the same day, Ariel Sharon appeared somewhat more conciliatory and stated, "To keep 3.5 million [Palestinian] people under occupation is bad for us and them."[8] In contrast, statements such as this, if followed by appropriate action, are much more likely to facilitate positive dialogue and assist in creating the climate necessary to achieve peace. Sharon's critics have argued that the conditional acceptance of the Road Map and Sharon's conciliatory remarks are a strategic move designed to deflect U.S,. pressure on Israel.[9] These critics point to Sharon's statement in early May 2003 when he maintained that renunciation of the Palestinian right of return "is something that Israel insists on and sees it as a condition for continuing the [peace] process."[10] This is an area of much contention. A great deal of dialogue and negotiation by both sides will be necessary to settle this important issue.

CONCLUSION

A March 28, 2003 *Jerusalem Times* editorial observed that "Israeli leaders have destroyed all bridges of trust and confidence between the Palestinian and Israeli people by their ill-fated and shortsighted policies." At the same time, it appears that the Palestinian Authority leadership has lost much credibility with the West for its internal corruption and failure to reign in militants.

As of June 2003, more than three thousand people have been killed and thousands more injured since the renewed uprising began in September 2000. These casualties have been on both sides. Innocent Palestinian and Israeli civilians have lost their lives. The death toll is rising rapidly. It is time for the leaders of both sides to put aside their differences and negotiate a lasting settlement. This lasting settlement should be rooted in the Oslo Peace Accords.

In addition to a lasting peace settlement with the Palestinians, peace, security, and mutual recognition between Israel with Syria and Lebanon should be sought after. From an economic standpoint, as well as a political standpoint, all parties stand to gain from a lasting peace settlement. Future agreements encompassing free trade and commerce would benefit Israelis as well as the Palestinians and neighboring Arab countries.

The Report of the Sharm El-Sheikh Fact-Finding Committee, which has become known as "The Mitchell Report," outlines a fair and comprehensive guideline for bringing the Israelis and Palestinians together to negotiate a permanent and lasting peace settlement that guarantees Israel's security while acknowledging the right of the Palestinians to self-autonomy and eventually, statehood. The Bush Administration's Quartet Plan Road Map To Peace, which is really a follow-up to the Mitchell Report, also offers a workable solution to facilitate dialogue and a peace agreement. There are extremists on both sides who do not want peace and oppose a permanent settlement between Israelis and Palestinians. I believe that these elements constitute a small minority. On the Palestinian side, some of the militant members and leaders of Hamas and Islamic Jihad are an obstacle since they oppose peace with Israel. Also, the corrupt practices of the Palestinian Authority need to be addressed. On the Israeli side, some ultra-conservatives, including Prime Minister Ariel Sharon, whose past policies have further instigated tensions, are an obstacle to achieving a lasting peace. The overwhelming majority of Israelis and Palestinians do support a lasting peace settlement that guarantees autonomy, independence, cooperation, and security for both sides. A very large percentage of Arab and Jewish Americans have expressed support for peace as well. In a poll conducted by Americans For Peace Now [APN], nearly eighty-seven percent of Jewish Americans and ninety-seven percent of Arab Americans agreed that Israelis and Palestinians each have the right to live in a secure and independent state of their own.[1]

To recap, a permanent peace settlement between Israelis and Palestinians must include an agreement acceptable to both sides addressing the following issues:

1. **Recognition of and security guarantees for Israel**

2. **The return of Palestinian refugees**

3. **The status and removal of certain Israeli settlements in the West Bank and Gaza Strip;**

4. **The creation of an independent and sovereign Palestinian state with its own government and police force**

5. **An agreement on the status of Jerusalem that acknowledges and respects the religious significance of this great city to Jews, Muslims, and Christians**

All of these elements were cited in the Oslo Peace Accords. Only when both sides set out to resolve these issues seriously can there be a lasting peace settlement.

Since 1996, both the Israeli government and the Palestinian Authority have breached provisions of the Oslo Accords. The Palestinians failed to halt propaganda against Israel in the Palestinian media, did not confiscate illegal firearms from Palestinian police and militants, engaged in corrupt government practices, and did not demonstrate enough force in fighting terrorism from extremists. The Netanyahu regime in Israel, which lasted form 1996 to 1999, further sabotaged the peace process and the Oslo Accords by expanding Israeli settlements and refusing to fully implement self-rule provisions in the Oslo Accords. This trend continued under Barak's Administration and now continue under Prime Minister Ariel Sharon. More than two hundred and seventy new Israeli settlements have been built in the occupied territories since the beginnings of the Oslo Peace Accords.

The Palestinian Authority must accept responsibility for not being forceful enough in preventing militant Palestinian extremists from initiating terrorist attacks against Israel. The Israelis, on the other hand, did not implement all of the stages of redeployment, failed to withdraw from territories that were supposed to be handed over to the Palestinians, worked to weaken the Palestinian Authority police force, and increased the amount of Israeli settlements on Palestinian territories.

In addition, Sharon is disregarding the Oslo Peace Accords, refusing to meet with leaders of the Palestinian Authority to resolve the conflict, and engaging in targeted assassinations of Palestinian resistance leaders. Even though the Palestinian Authority leadership leaves much to be desired in terms of its own governance, it still remains the sole representative of the Palestinian people as recognized by the Arab states and by Israel through previous declarations. Therefore, it is counterproductive not to engage the leaders of the Palestinian Authority in dialogue. Ariel Sharon's policies as Prime Minister have clearly escalated tensions. Despite pressure from the United States to do otherwise, Sharon has engaged in the expansion of Israeli settlements in Palestinian territories and has pursued a policy of demolishing Palestinian homes and villages leaving hundreds of Palestinian civilians homeless and destitute. These actions are a root cause of the unfortunate and widespread, but unjustifiable, suicide bombings that we continue to witness in this region. Sharon himself has stated consistently, "I never accepted the Oslo agreement as it was." On the campaign trail for Prime Minister, Sharon again declared, "The Oslo agreement is finished. It doesn't exist." Statements such as these only incite protest and do little to advance the peace process.

In a March 29, 2002 *CNN* interview, Former National Security Advisor and Chairman of the Trilateral Commission Zbigniew Brzezinski observed, "For the past 10 years, Mr. Sharon has opposed the Oslo peace process…and has worked to undermine the Palestinian Authority." The "peace" that Ariel Sharon wants is incompatible with the peace that the Palestinian people require. Sharon wants to continue occupying and exploiting the Palestinians but still wants to end the violence. This is just as unrealistic and unacceptable as the radical Islamic Jihad's peace plan which encompasses the complete destruction of the State of Israel. In the eyes of the Palestinian people, the Israeli government encompasses a conquering army in the West Bank and Gaza Strip. Palestinian land can be taken at will, family homes demolished, citizens jailed for no reason and without trial, and curfews can be imposed on the entire population. Parallels can easily be drawn between the current state of the Palestinian people and the state of the American colonists prior to the American Revolution.

On the other hand, suicide bombings and terrorist attacks from the Palestinian militant groups Hamas and Islamic Jihad only injure innocent civilians, ignite anger and protest, and serve to hurt chances for a lasting peace settlement. Like most people, I believe in the Palestinian cause for self-determination and statehood but not in the terrorist methods that some Palestinian militants are using to achieve it. The Palestinian people have every right not to be exploited but they cannot sanction the killing of innocent civilians and still expect to obtain world sympathy and support from the international community. Yasir Arafat and the Palestinian Authority need to be more forceful in condemning and arresting Palestinian militants who engage in terrorist activities against Israeli civilians. They also need to restore confidence in their management by reforming their corrupt practices.

The May 22, 2001 *Frankfurter Rundschow* of Germany observed, "Never since the Oslo Peace Accords has war seemed so likely." Britain's *Independent* of May 24, 2001 called Sharon's settlement expansions "unacceptable and implausible." The June 1, 2001 *Economist* stated that Sharon's settlement expansions "negate all chance of Palestinian-Israeli peaceful coexistence."

In August 2001, the Palestinian Authority repeated calls for international peacekeepers to be sent to monitor the West Bank and Gaza Strip. The Palestinian Authority has argued that only an international observer force can bring about a real cease-fire between Israelis and Palestinians. Prime Minister Sharon has rejected the use of international peacekeepers. Sharon states, "We will not be able to accept international forces or international observers." Sharon argues that an international peace force will restrict the movement of the Israeli military and be biased against Israel. A temporary voluntary international observer force may be necessary to help monitor a truce and make it possible to implement the provisions of the Mitchell Report, however, a lasting comprehensive peace settlement depends upon the commitment of both Israeli and Palestinian leaders to achieve peace. Despite his past, Ariel Sharon is in the perfect historical position to reach a lasting peace settlement between the Israelis and the Palestinians and Israel and her Arab neighbors. Let us hope that he seizes upon this opportunity to do so.

As the late Israeli Prime Minister Yitzhak Rabin, who gave his life in the name of peace, articulated so clearly during the signing of the Oslo Accords "enough blood and tears." The Oslo Accords encompass the link between the end of war and the era of peace. Let us hope and pray that the leaders of both sides will find the courage to put aside past animosity, to develop a positive vision for the future, and lead their peoples into a new era of peace, security, economic cooperation, and coexistence based upon mutual respect for traditions, religions, and cultures.

APPENDIX A

The Oslo Agreement: Declaration Of Principles On Interim Self-Government Arrangements

September 13, 1993

The Government of the State of Israel and the P.L.O. team (in the Jordanian-Palestinian delegation to the Middle East Peace Conference) (the "Palestinian Delegation"), representing the Palestinian people, agree that it is time to put an end to decades of confrontation and conflict, recognize their mutual legitimate and political rights, and strive to live in peaceful coexistence and mutual dignity and security and achieve a just, lasting and comprehensive peace settlement and historic reconciliation through the agreed political process. Accordingly, the, two sides agree to the following principles:

ARTICLE I

AIM OF THE NEGOTIATIONS

The aim of the Israeli-Palestinian negotiations within the current Middle East peace process is, among other things, to establish a Palestinian Interim Self-Government Authority, the elected Council (the "Council"), for the Palestinian people in the West Bank and the Gaza Strip, for a transitional period not exceeding five years, leading to a permanent settlement based on Security Council Resolutions 242 and 338.

It is understood that the interim arrangements are an integral part of the whole peace process and that the negotiations on the permanent status will lead to the implementation of Security Council Resolutions 242 and 338.

ARTICLE II

FRAMEWORK FOR THE INTERIM PERIOD

The agreed framework for the interim period is set forth in this Declaration of Principles.

ARTICLE III

ELECTIONS

In order that the Palestinian people in the West Bank and Gaza Strip may govern themselves according to democratic principles, direct, free and general political elections will be held for the Council under agreed supervision and international observation, while the Palestinian police will ensure public order.

An agreement will be concluded on the exact mode and conditions of the elections in accordance with the protocol attached as Annex I, with the goal of holding the elections not later than nine months after the entry into force of this Declaration of Principles.

These elections will constitute a significant interim preparatory step toward the realization of the legitimate rights of the Palestinian people and their just requirements.

ARTICLE IV

JURISDICTION

Jurisdiction of the Council will cover West Bank and Gaza Strip territory, except for issues that will be negotiated in the permanent status negotiations. The two sides view the West Bank and the Gaza Strip as a single territorial unit, whose integrity will be preserved during the interim period.

ARTICLE V

TRANSITIONAL PERIOD AND PERMANENT STATUS NEGOTIATIONS

The five-year transitional period will begin upon the withdrawal from the Gaza Strip and Jericho area.

Permanent status negotiations will commence as soon as possible, but not later than the beginning of the third year of the interim period, between the Government of Israel and the Palestinian people representatives.

It is understood that these negotiations shall cover remaining issues, including: Jerusalem, refugees, settlements, security arrangements, borders, relations and cooperation with other neighbors, and other issues of common interest.

The two parties agree that the outcome of the permanent status negotiations should not be prejudiced or preempted by agreements reached for the interim period.

ARTICLE VI

PREPARATORY TRANSFER OF POWERS AND RESPONSIBILITIES

Upon the entry into force of this Declaration of Principles and the withdrawal from the Gaza Strip and the Jericho area, a transfer of authority from the Israeli military government and its Civil Administration to the authorised Palestinians for this task, as detailed herein, will commence. This transfer of authority will be of a preparatory nature until the inauguration of the Council.

Immediately after the entry into force of this Declaration of Principles and the withdrawal from the Gaza Strip and Jericho area, with the view to promoting economic development in the West Bank and Gaza Strip, authority will be transferred to the Palestinians on the following spheres: education and culture, health, social welfare, direct taxation, and tourism. The Palestinian side will commence in building the Palestinian police force, as agreed upon. Pending the inauguration of the Council, the two parties may negotiate the transfer of additional powers and responsibilities, as agreed upon.

ARTICLE VII

INTERIM AGREEMENT

The Israeli and Palestinian delegations will negotiate an agreement on the interim period (the "Interim Agreement")

The Interim Agreement shall specify, among other things, the structure of the Council, the number of its members, and the transfer of powers and responsibilities from the Israeli military government and its Civil Administration to the Council. The Interim Agreement shall also specify the Council's executive authority, legislative authority in accordance with Article IX below, and the independent Palestinian judicial organs.
The Interim Agreement shall include arrangements, to be implemented upon the inauguration of the Council, for the assumption by the Council of all of the powers and responsibilities transferred previously in accordance with Article VI above.
In order to enable the Council to promote economic growth, upon its inauguration, the Council will establish, among other things, a Palestinian Electricity Authority, a Gaza Sea Port Authority, a Palestinian Development Bank, a Palestinian Export Promotion Board, a Palestinian Environmental Authority, a Palestinian Land Authority and a Palestinian Water Administration Authority, and any other Authorities agreed upon, in accordance with the Interim Agreement that will specify their powers and responsibilities.

After the inauguration of the Council, the Civil Administration will be dissolved, and the Israeli military government will be withdrawn.

ARTICLE VIII

PUBLIC ORDER AND SECURITY

In order to guarantee public order and internal security for the Palestinians of the West Bank and the Gaza Strip, the Council will establish a strong police force, while Israel will continue to carry the responsibility for defending against external threats, as well as the responsibility for overall security of Israelis for the purpose of safeguarding their internal security and public order.

ARTICLE IX

LAWS AND MILITARY ORDERS

The Council will be empowered to legislate, in accordance with the Interim Agreement, within all authorities transferred to it.

Both parties will review jointly laws and military orders presently in force in remaining spheres.

ARTICLE X

JOINT ISRAELI-PALESTINIAN LIAISON COMMITTEE

In order to provide for a smooth implementation of this Declaration of Principles and any subsequent agreements pertaining to the interim period, upon the entry into force of this Declaration of Principles, a Joint Israeli-Palestinian Liaison Committee will be established in order to deal with issues requiring coordination, other issues of common interest, and disputes.

ARTICLE XI

ISRAELI-PALESTINIAN COOPERATION IN ECONOMIC FIELDS

Recognizing the mutual benefit of cooperation in promoting the development of the West Bank, the Gaza Strip and Israel, upon the entry into force of this Declaration of Principles, an Israeli-Palestinian Economic Cooperation Committee will be established in order to develop and implement in a cooperative manner the programs identified in the protocols attached as Annex III and Annex IV .

ARTICLE XII

LIAISON AND COOPERATION WITH JORDAN AND EGYPT

The two parties will invite the Governments of Jordan and Egypt to participate in establishing further liaison and cooperation arrangements between the Government of Israel and the Palestinian representatives, on the one hand, and the

Governments of Jordan and Egypt, on the other hand, to promote cooperation between them. These arrangements will include the constitution of a Continuing Committee that will decide by agreement on the modalities of admission of persons displaced from the West Bank and Gaza Strip in 1967, together with necessary measures to prevent disruption and disorder. Other matters of common concern will be dealt with by this Committee.

ARTICLE XIII

REDEPLOYMENT OF ISRAELI FORCES

After the entry into force of this Declaration of Principles, and not later than the eve of elections for the Council, a redeployment of Israeli military forces in the West Bank and the Gaza Strip will take place, in addition to withdrawal of Israeli forces carried out in accordance with Article XIV.

In redeploying its military forces, Israel will be guided by the principle that its military forces should be redeployed outside populated areas.

Further redeployments to specified locations will be gradually implemented commensurate with the assumption of responsibility for public order and internal security by the Palestinian police force pursuant to Article VIII above.

ARTICLE XIV

ISRAELI WITHDRAWAL FROM THE GAZA STRIP AND JERICHO AREA

Israel will withdraw from the Gaza Strip and Jericho area, as detailed in the protocol attached as Annex II.

ARTICLE XV

RESOLUTION OF DISPUTES

Disputes arising out of the application or interpretation of this Declaration of Principles. or any subsequent agreements pertaining to the interim period, shall be resolved by negotiations through the Joint Liaison Committee to be established pursuant to Article X above.

Disputes which cannot be settled by negotiations may be resolved by a mechanism of conciliation to be agreed upon by the parties.

The parties may agree to submit to arbitration disputes relating to the interim period, which cannot be settled through conciliation. To this end, upon the agreement of both parties, the parties will establish an Arbitration Committee.

ARTICLE XVI

ISRAELI-PALESTINIAN COOPERATION CONCERNING REGIONAL PROGRAMS

Both parties view the multilateral working groups as an appropriate instrument for promoting a "Marshall Plan", the regional programs and other programs, including special programs for the West Bank and Gaza Strip, as indicated in the protocol attached as Annex IV .

ARTICLE XVII

MISCELLANEOUS PROVISIONS

This Declaration of Principles will enter into force one month after its signing.

All protocols annexed to this Declaration of Principles and Agreed Minutes pertaining thereto shall be regarded as an integral part hereof.

Done at Washington, D.C., this thirteenth day of September, 1993.
For the Government of Israel
For the P.L.O.

Witnessed By:
The United States of America
The Russian Federation

ANNEX I
PROTOCOL ON THE MODE AND
CONDITIONS OF ELECTIONS

Palestinians of Jerusalem who live there will have the right to participate in the election process, according to an agreement between the two sides.

In addition, the election agreement should cover, among other things, the following issues:

> the system of elections;

> the mode of the agreed supervision and international observation and their personal composition; and

> rules and regulations regarding election campaign, including agreed arrangements for the organizing of mass media, and the possibility of licensing a broadcasting and TV station.

The future status of displaced Palestinians who were registered on 4th June 1967 will not be prejudiced because they are unable to participate in the election process due to practical reasons.

ANNEX II
PROTOCOL ON WITHDRAWAL OF
ISRAELI FORCES FROM THE GAZA STRIP
AND JERICHO AREA

The two sides will conclude and sign within two months from the date of entry into force of this Declaration of Principles, an agreement on the withdrawal of Israeli military forces from the Gaza Strip and Jericho area. This agreement will include comprehensive arrangements to apply in the Gaza Strip and the Jericho area subsequent to the Israeli withdrawal.

Israel will implement an accelerated and scheduled withdrawal of Israeli military forces from the Gaza Strip and Jericho area, beginning immediately with the signing of the agreement on the Gaza Strip and Jericho area and to be completed within a period not exceeding four months after the signing of this agreement.

The above agreement will include, among other things:

Arrangements for a smooth and peaceful transfer of authority from the Israeli military government and its Civil Administration to the Palestinian representatives.

Structure, powers and responsibilities of the Palestinian authority in these areas, except: external security, settlements, Israelis, foreign relations, and other mutually agreed matters.

Arrangements for the assumption of internal security and public order by the Palestinian police force consisting of police officers recruited locally and from abroad holding Jordanian passports and Palestinian documents issued by Egypt). Those who will participate in the Palestinian police force coming from abroad should be trained as police and police officers.

A temporary international or foreign presence, as agreed upon.

Establishment of a joint Palestinian-Israeli Coordination and Cooperation Committee for mutual security purposes.

An economic development and stabilization program, including the establishment of an Emergency Fund, to encourage foreign investment, and financial and economic support. Both sides will coordinate and cooperate jointly and unilaterally with regional and international parties to support these aims.

Arrangements for a safe passage for persons and transportation between the Gaza Strip and Jericho area.

The above agreement will include arrangements for coordination between both parties regarding passages:

Gaza—Egypt; and

Jericho—Jordan.

The offices responsible for carrying out the powers and responsibilities of the Palestinian authority under this Annex II and Article VI of the Declaration of Principles will be located in the Gaza Strip and in the Jericho area pending the inauguration of the Council.

Other than these agreed arrangements, the status of the Gaza Strip and Jericho area will continue to be an integral part of the West Bank and Gaza Strip, and will not be changed in the interim period.

ANNEX III
PROTOCOL ON ISRAELI-PALESTINIAN COOPERATION IN ECONOMIC AND DEVELOPMENT PROGRAMS

The two sides agree to establish an Israeli-Palestinian continuing Committee for Economic Cooperation, focusing, among other things, on the following:

Cooperation in the field of water, including a Water Development Program prepared by experts from both sides, which will also specify the mode of cooperation in the management of water resources in the West Bank and Gaza Strip, and will include proposals for studies and plans on water rights of each party, as well as on the equitable utilization of joint water resources for implementation in and beyond the interim period.

Cooperation in the field of electricity, including an Electricity Development Program, which will also specify the mode of cooperation for the production, maintenance, purchase and sale of electricity resources.

Cooperation in the field of energy, including an Energy Development Program, which will provide for the exploitation of oil and gas for industrial purposes, particularly in the Gaza Strip and in the Negev, and will encourage further joint exploitation of other energy resources. This Program may also provide for the construction of a Petrochemical industrial complex in the Gaza Strip and the construction of oil and gas pipelines.

Cooperation in the field of finance, including a Financial Development and Action Program for the encouragement of international investment in the West Bank and the Gaza Strip, and in Israel, as well as the establishment of a Palestinian Development Bank.

Cooperation in the field of transport and communications, including a Program, which will define guidelines for the establishment of a Gaza Sea Port Area, and will provide for the establishing of transport and communications lines to and from the West Bank and the Gaza Strip to Israel and to other countries. In addition, this Program will provide for carrying out the necessary construction of roads, railways, communications lines, etc.

Cooperation in the field of trade, including studies, and Trade Promotion Programs, which will encourage local, regional and inter-regional trade, as well as a feasibility study of creating free trade zones in the Gaza Strip and in Israel, mutual access to these zones, and cooperation in other areas related to trade and commerce.

Cooperation in the field of industry, including Industrial Development Programs, which will provide for the establishment of joint Israeli-Palestinian Industrial Research and Development Centers, will promote Palestinian-Israeli joint ventures, and provide guidelines for cooperation in the textile, food, pharmaceutical, electronics, diamonds, computer and science-based industries.

A program for cooperation in, and regulation of, labor relations and cooperation in social welfare issues.

A Human Resources Development and Cooperation Plan, providing for joint Israeli-Palestinian workshops and seminars, and for the establishment of joint vocational training centers, research institutes and data banks.

An Environmental Protection Plan, providing for joint and/or coordinated measures in this sphere.

A program for developing coordination and cooperation in the field of communication and media.

Any other programs of mutual interest.

ANNEX IV
PROTOCOL ON ISRAELI-PALESTINIAN COOPERATION CONCERNING REGIONAL DEVELOPMENT PROGRAMS

The two sides will cooperate in the context of the multilateral peace efforts in promoting a Development Program for the region, including the West Bank and the Gaza Strip, to be initiated by the G-7. The parties will request the G-7 to seek the participation in this program of other interested states, such as members of the Organisation for Economic Cooperation and Development, regional Arab states and institutions, as well as members of the private sector.

The Development Program will consist of two elements:

an Economic Development Program for the 'West Bank and the Gaza Strip.

a Regional Economic Development Program.

The Economic Development Program for the West Bank and the Gaza strip will consist of the following elements:

A Social Rehabilitation Program, including a Housing and Construction Program.

A Small and Medium Business Development Plan.

An Infrastructure Development Program (water, electricity, transportation and communications, etc.)

A Human Resources Plan.

Other programs.

The Regional Economic Development Program may consist of the following elements:

The establishment of a Middle East Development Fund, as a first step, and a Middle East Development Bank, as a second step.

The development of a joint Israeli-Palestinian-Jordanian Plan for coordinated exploitation of the Dead Sea area.

The Mediterranean Sea (Gaza)—Dead Sea Canal.

Regional Desalinization and other water development projects.

A regional plan for agricultural development, including a coordinated regional effort for the prevention of desertification.

Interconnection of electricity grids.

Regional cooperation for the transfer, distribution and industrial exploitation of gas, oil and other energy resources.

A Regional Tourism, Transportation and Telecommunications Development Plan.

Regional cooperation in other spheres.

The two sides will encourage the multilateral working groups, and will coordinate towards their success. The two parties will encourage intersessional activities, as well as pre-feasibility and feasibility studies, within the various multilateral working groups.

AGREED MINUTES TO THE DECLARATION OF PRINCIPLES ON INTERIM SELF-GOVERNMENT ARRANGEMENTS

A. GENERAL UNDERSTANDINGS AND AGREEMENTS

Any powers and responsibilities transferred to the Palestinians pursuant to the Declaration of Principles prior to the inauguration of the Council will be subject to the same principles pertaining to Article IV, as set out in these Agreed Minutes below.

B. SPECIFIC UNDERSTANDINGS AND AGREEMENTS

Article IV

It is understood that:

Jurisdiction of the Council will cover West Bank and Gaza Strip territory, except for issues that will be negotiated in the permanent status negotiations: Jerusalem, settlements, military locations, and Israelis.

The Council's jurisdiction will apply with regard to the agreed powers, responsibilities, spheres and authorities transferred to it.

Article VI (2)

It is agreed that the transfer of authority will be as follows:

> The Palestinian side will inform the Israeli side of the names of the authorised Palestinians who will assume the powers, authorities and responsibilities that will be transferred to the Palestinians according to the Declaration of Principles in the following fields: education and culture, health, social welfare, direct taxation, tourism, and any other authorities agreed upon.

> It is understood that the rights and obligations of these offices will not be affected.

> Each of the spheres described above will continue to enjoy existing budgetary allocations in accordance with arrangements to be mutually agreed upon. These arrangements also will provide for the necessary adjustments required in order to take into account the taxes collected by the direct taxation office.

> Upon the execution of the Declaration of Principles, the Israeli and Palestinian delegations will immediately commence negotiations on a detailed plan for the transfer of authority on the above offices in accordance with the above understandings.

Article VII (2)

The Interim Agreement will also include arrangements for coordination and cooperation.

Article VII (5)

The withdrawal of the military government will not prevent Israel from exercising the powers and responsibilities not transferred to the Council.

Article VIII

It is understood that the Interim Agreement will include arrangements for cooperation and coordination between the two parties in this regard. It is also agreed that the transfer of powers and responsibilities to the Palestinian police will be accomplished in a phased manner, as agreed in the Interim Agreement.

Article X

It is agreed that, upon the entry into force of the Declaration of Principles, the Israeli and Palestinian delegations will exchange the names of the individuals designated by them as members of the Joint Israeli-Palestinian Liaison Committee.

It is further agreed that each side will have an equal number of members in the Joint Committee. The Joint Committee will reach decisions by agreement. The Joint Committee may add other technicians and experts, as necessary. The Joint Committee will decide on the frequency and place or places of its meetings.

Annex II

It is understood that, subsequent to the Israeli withdrawal, Israel will continue to be responsible for external security, and for internal security and public order of settlements and Israelis. Israeli military forces and civilians may continue to use roads freely within the Gaza Strip and the Jericho area.

Done at Washington, D.C., this thirteenth day of September, 1993.
For the Government of Israel
For the P.L.O.
Witnessed By:
The United States of America
The Russian Federation

APPENDIX B

Text Of The Mitchell Report: Report Of The Sharm El-Sheikh Fact-Finding Committee

The following is the full text of the report completed on April 30, 2001 and published on May 20, 2001.

SUMMARY OF RECOMMENDATIONS

The Government of Israel (GOI) and the Palestinian Authority (PA) must act swiftly and decisively to halt the violence. Their immediate objectives then should be to rebuild confidence and resume negotiations.

During this mission our aim has been to fulfill the mandate agreed at Sharm el-Sheikh.

We value the support given our work by the participants at the summit, and we commend the parties for their cooperation. Our principal recommendation is that they recommit themselves to the Sharm el-Sheikh spirit and that they implement the decisions made there in 1999 and 2000. We believe that the summit participants will support bold action by the parties to achieve these objectives.

The restoration of trust is essential, and the parties should take affirmative steps to this end. Given the high level of hostility and mistrust, the timing and sequence of these steps are obviously crucial. This can be decided only by the parties. We urge them to begin the process of decision immediately.

Accordingly, we recommend that steps be taken to:

END THE VIOLENCE

- The GOI and the PA should reaffirm their commitment to existing agreements and undertakings and should immediately implement an unconditional cessation of violence.

- The GOI and PA should immediately resume security cooperation.

REBUILD CONFIDENCE

- The PA and GOI should work together to establish a meaningful "cooling off period" and implement additional confidence building measures, some of which were detailed in the October 2000 Sharm el-Sheikh Statement and some of which were offered by the U.S. on January 7, 2001 in Cairo (see Recommendations section for further description).

- The PA and GOI should resume their efforts to identify, condemn and discourage incitement in all its forms.

- The PA should make clear through concrete action to Palestinians and Israelis alike that terrorism is reprehensible and unacceptable, and that the PA will make a 100 percent effort to prevent terrorist operations and to punish perpetrators. This effort should include immediate steps to apprehend and incarcerate terrorists operating within the PA's jurisdiction.

- The GOI should freeze all settlement activity, including the "natural growth" of existing settlements.

- The GOI should ensure that the IDF adopt and enforce policies and procedures encouraging non-lethal responses to unarmed demonstrators, with a view to minimizing casualties and friction between the two communities.

- The PA should prevent gunmen from using Palestinian populated areas to fire upon Israeli populated areas and IDF positions. This tactic places civilians on both sides at unnecessary risk.

- The GOI should lift closures, transfer to the PA all tax revenues owed, and permit Palestinians who had been employed in Israel to return to their jobs; and should ensure that security forces and settlers refrain from the destruction of homes and roads, as well as trees and other agricultural property in Palestin-

ian areas. We acknowledge the GOI's position that actions of this nature have been taken for security reasons.
Nevertheless, the economic effects will persist for years.

- The PA should renew cooperation with Israeli security agencies to ensure, to the maximum extent possible, that Palestinian workers employed within Israel are fully vetted and free of connections to organizations and individuals engaged in terrorism.

- The PA and GOI should consider a joint undertaking to preserve and protect holy places sacred to the traditions of Jews, Muslims, and Christians.

- The GOI and PA should jointly endorse and support the work of Palestinian and Israeli non-governmental organizations involved in cross-community initiatives linking the two peoples.

RESUME NEGOTIATIONS

- In the spirit of the Sharm el-Sheikh agreements and understandings of 1999 and 2000, we recommend that the parties meet to reaffirm their commitment to signed agreements and mutual understandings, and take corresponding action.
This should be the basis for resuming full and meaningful negotiations.

INTRODUCTION

On October 17, 2000, at the conclusion of the Middle East Peace Summit at Sharm el-Sheikh, Egypt, the President of the United States spoke on behalf of the participants (the Government of Israel, the Palestinian Authority, the Governments of Egypt, Jordan, and the United States, the United Nations, and the European Union). Among other things, the President stated that: The United States will develop with the Israelis and Palestinians, as well as in consultation with the United Nations Secretary General, a committee of fact-finding on the events of the past several weeks and how to prevent their recurrence. The committee's report will be shared by the U.S.

President with the U.N. Secretary General and the parties prior to publication. A final report shall be submitted under the auspices of the U.S. President for publication.[1]

On November 7, 2000, following consultations with the other participants, the President asked us to serve on what has come to be known as the Sharm el-Sheikh Fact-Finding Committee. In a letter to us on December 6, 2000, the President stated that: The purpose of the Summit, and of the agreement that ensued, was to end the violence, to prevent its recurrence, and to find a path back to the peace process. In its actions and mode of operation, therefore, the Committee should be guided by these overriding goals. The Committee should strive to steer clear of any step that will intensify mutual blame and finger-pointing between the parties. As I noted in my previous letter, "the Committee should not become a divisive force or a focal point for blame and recrimination but rather should serve to forestall violence and confrontation and provide lessons for the future." This should not be a tribunal whose purpose is to determine the guilt or innocence of individuals or of the parties; rather, it should be a fact-finding committee whose purpose is to determine what happened and how to avoid it recurring in the future.[2]

After our first meeting, held before we visited the region, we urged an end to all violence. Our meetings and our observations during our subsequent visits to the region have intensified our convictions in this regard.

Whatever the source, violence will not solve the problems of the region. It will only make them worse. Death and destruction will not bring peace, but will deepen the hatred and harden the resolve on both sides. There is only one way to peace, justice, and security in the Middle East, and that is through negotiation.

Despite their long history and close proximity, some Israelis and Palestinians seem not to fully appreciate each other's problems and concerns. Some Israelis appear not to comprehend the humiliation and frustration that Palestinians must endure every day as a result of living with the continuing effects of occupation, sustained by the presence of Israeli military forces and settlements in their midst, or the determination of the Palestinians to achieve independence and genuine self-determination.

Some Palestinians appear not to comprehend the extent to which terrorism creates fear among the Israeli people and undermines their belief in the possibility of co-existence, or the determination of the GOI to do whatever is necessary to protect its people.

Fear, hate, anger, and frustration have risen on both sides. The greatest danger of all is that the culture of peace, nurtured over the previous decade, is being shattered. In its place there is a growing sense of futility and despair, and a growing resort to violence.

Political leaders on both sides must act and speak decisively to reverse these dangerous trends; they must rekindle the desire and the drive for peace. That will be difficult. But it can be done and it must be done, for the alternative is unacceptable and should be unthinkable.

Two proud peoples share a land and a destiny. Their competing claims and religious differences have led to a grinding, demoralizing, dehumanizing conflict. They can continue in conflict or they can negotiate to find a way to live side-by-side in peace.

There is a record of achievement. In 1991 the first peace conference with Israelis and Palestinians took place in Madrid to achieve peace based on UN Security Council Resolutions 242 and 338. In 1993, the Palestine Liberation Organization (PLO) and Israel met in Oslo for the first face-to-face negotiations; they led to mutual recognition and the Declaration of Principles (signed by the parties in Washington, D.C. on September 13, 1993), which provided a road map to reach the destination agreed in Madrid. Since then, important steps have been taken in Cairo, in Washington, and elsewhere. Last year the parties came very close to a permanent settlement.

So much has been achieved. So much is at risk. If the parties are to succeed in completing their journey to their common destination, agreed commitments must be implemented, international law respected, and human rights protected. We encourage them to return to negotiations, however difficult.

It is the only path to peace, justice and security.

DISCUSSION

It is clear from their statements that the participants in the summit of last October hoped and intended that the outbreak of violence, then less than a month old, would soon end. The U.S. President's letters to us, asking that we make recommendations on how to prevent a recurrence of violence, reflect that intention.

Yet the violence has not ended. It has worsened. Thus the overriding concern of those in the region with whom we spoke is to end the violence and to return to the process of shaping a sustainable peace. That is what we were told, and were asked to address, by Israelis and Palestinians alike. It was the message conveyed to us as well by President Mubarak of Egypt, King Abdullah of Jordan, and UN Secretary General Annan.

Their concern must be ours. If our report is to have effect, it must deal with the situation that exists, which is different from that envisaged by the summit participants.

In this report, we will try to answer the questions assigned to us by the Sharm el-Sheikh summit: What happened? Why did it happen? In light of the current situation, however, we must elaborate on the third part of our mandate: How can the recurrence of violence be prevented? The relevance and impact of our work, in the end, will be measured by the recommendations we make concerning the following:

- Ending the Violence.

- Rebuilding Confidence.

- Resuming Negotiations.

WHAT HAPPENED?

We are not a tribunal. We complied with the request that we not determine the guilt or innocence of individuals or of the parties. We did not have the power to compel the testimony of witnesses or the production of documents.

Most of the information we received came from the parties and, understandably, it largely tended to support their arguments.

In this part of our report, we do not attempt to chronicle all of the events from late September 2000 onward. Rather, we discuss only those that shed light on the underlying causes of violence.

In late September 2000, Israeli, Palestinian, and other officials received reports that Member of the Knesset (now Prime Minister) Ariel Sharon was planning a visit to the Haram al Sharif/Temple Mount in Jerusalem.

Palestinian and U.S. officials urged then Prime Minister Ehud Barak to prohibit the visit.[3] Mr. Barak told us that he believed the visit was intended to be an internal political act directed against him by a political opponent, and he declined to prohibit it.

Mr. Sharon made the visit on September 28 accompanied by over 1,000 Israeli police officers. Although Israelis viewed the visit in an internal political context, Palestinians saw it as highly provocative to them. On the following day, in the same place, a large number of unarmed Palestinian demonstrators and a large Israeli police contingent confronted each other. According to the U.S.

Department of State, "Palestinians held large demonstrations and threw stones at police in the vicinity of the Western Wall. Police used rubber-coated metal bullets and live ammunition to disperse the demonstrators, killing 4 persons and injuring about 200."[4] According to the GOI, 14 Israeli policemen were injured.[5] Similar demonstrations took place over the following several days.[6] Thus began what has become known as the "Al-Aqsa Intifada" (Al-Aqsa being a mosque at the Haram al-Sharif/Temple Mount).

The GOI asserts that the immediate catalyst for the violence was the breakdown of the Camp David negotiations on July 25, 2000 and the "widespread appreciation in the international community of Palestinian responsibility for the impasse. In this view, Palestinian violence was planned by the PA leadership, and was aimed at "provoking and incurring Palestinian casualties as a means of regaining the diplomatic initiative."[8] The Palestine Liberation Organization (PLO) denies the allegation that the intifada was planned. it claims, however, that "Camp David represented nothing less than an attempt by Israel to extend the force it exercises on the ground to negotiations,"[9] and that "the failure of the summit, and the attempts to allocate blame on the Palestinian side only added to the tension on the ground...[10]

From the perspective of the PLO, Israel responded to the disturbances with excessive and illegal use of deadly force against demonstrators; behavior which, in the PLO's view, reflected Israel's contempt for the lives and safety of Palestinians. For Palestinians, the widely seen images of the killing of 12-year-old Muhammad al Durra in Gaza on September 30, shot as he huddled behind his father, reinforced that perception.

From the perspective of the GOI, the demonstrations were organized and directed by the Palestinian leadership to create sympathy for their cause around the world by provoking Israeli security forces to fire upon demonstrators, especially young people. For Israelis, the lynching of two military reservists, First Sgt. Vadim Novesche and First Cpl. Yosef Avrahami, in Ramallah on October 12, reflected a deep-seated Palestinian hatred of Israel and Jews.

What began as a series of confrontations between Palestinian demonstrators and Israeli security forces, which resulted in the GOI's initial restrictions on the movement of people and goods in the West Bank and Gaza Strip (closures), has since evolved into a wider array of violent actions and responses. There have been exchanges of fire between built-up areas, sniping incidents and clashes between Israeli settlers and Palestinians.

There have also been terrorist acts and Israeli reactions thereto (characterized by the GOI as counter-terrorism). including killings, further destruction of property and economic measures. Most recently, there have been mortar attacks on Israeli locations and IDF ground incursions into Palestinian areas.

From the Palestinian perspective, the decision of Israel to characterize the current crisis as "an armed conflict short of war"[11] is simply a means "to justify its assassination policy, its collective punishment policy, and its use of lethal force."[12] From the Israeli perspective, "The Palestinian leadership have instigated, orchestrated and directed the violence. It has used, and continues to use, terror and attrition as strategic tools."[13] In their submissions, the parties traded allegations about the motivation and degree of control exercised by the other. However, we were provided with no persuasive evidence that the Sharon visit was anything other than an internal political act; neither were we provided with persuasive evidence that the PA planned the uprising.

Accordingly, we have no basis on which to conclude that there was a deliberate plan by the PA to initiate a campaign of violence at the first opportunity; or to conclude that there was a deliberate plan by the GOI to respond with lethal force.

However, there is also no evidence on which to conclude that the PA made a consistent effort to contain the demonstrations and control the violence once it began; or that the GOI made a consistent effort to use non-lethal means to control demonstrations of unarmed Palestinians. Amid rising anger, fear, and mistrust, each side assumed the worst about the other and acted accordingly.

The Sharon visit did not cause the "Al-Aqsa Initifada." But it was poorly timed and the provocative effect should have been foreseen; indeed it was foreseen by those who urged that the visit be prohibited. More significant were the events that followed: the decision of the Israeli police on September 29 to use lethal means against the Palestinian demonstrators; and the subsequent failure, as noted above, of either party to exercise restraint.

WHY DID IT HAPPEN?

The roots of the current violence extend much deeper than an inconclusive summit conference. Both sides have made clear a profound disillusionment with the behavior of the other in failing to meet the expectations arising from the peace process launched in Madrid in 1991 and then in Oslo in 1993.

Each side has accused the other of violating specific undertakings and undermining the spirit of their commitment to resolving their political differences peacefully.

Divergent Expectations: We are struck by the divergent expectations expressed by the parties relating to the implementation of the Oslo process.

Results achieved from this process were unthinkable less than 10 years ago.

During the latest round of negotiations, the parties were closer to a permanent settlement than ever before.

Nonetheless, Palestinians and Israelis alike told us that the premise on which the Oslo process is based—that tackling the hard "permanent status" issues be deferred to the end of the process has gradually come under serious pressure. The step-by-step process agreed to by the parties was based on the assumption that each step in the negotiating process would lead to enhanced trust and confidence. To achieve this, each party would have to implement agreed-upon commitments and abstain from actions that would be seen by the other as attempts to abuse the process in order to predetermine the shape of the final outcome. If this requirement is not met, the Oslo road map cannot successfully lead to its agreed destination. Today, each side blames the other for having ignored this fundamental aspect, resulting in a crisis in confidence. This problem became even more pressing with the opening of permanent status talks.

The GOI has placed primacy on moving toward a Permanent Status Agreement in a nonviolent atmosphere, consistent with commitments contained in the agreements between the parties. "Even if slower than was initially envisaged, there has, since the start of the peace process in Madrid in 1991, been steady progress towards the goal of a Permanent Status Agreement without the resort to violence on a scale that has characterized recent weeks."[14] The "goal" is the Permanent Status Agreement, the terms of which must be negotiated by the parties.

The PLO view is that delays in the process have been the result of an Israeli attempt to prolong and solidify the occupation. Palestinians "believed that the Oslo process would yield an end to Israeli occupation in five years,"[15] the time-frame for the transitional period specified in the Declaration of Principles. Instead there have been, in the PLO's view, repeated Israeli delays culminating in the Camp David summit, where, "Israel proposed to annex about 11.2% of the West Bank (excluding Jerusalem)..." and offered unacceptable proposals concerning Jerusalem, security and refugees. "In sum, Israel's proposals at Camp David provided for Israel's annexation of the best Palestinian lands, the perpetuation of Israeli control over East Jerusalem. a continued Israeli military presence on Palestinian territory, Israeli control over Palestinian natural resources, airspace and borders, and the return of fewer than 1% of refugees to their homes."[16]

Both sides see the lack of full compliance with agreements reached since the opening of the peace process as evidence of a lack of good faith. This conclusion led to an erosion of trust even before the permanent status negotiations began.

Divergent Perspectives: During the last seven months, these views have hardened into divergent realities. Each side views the other as having acted in bad faith; as having turned the optimism of Oslo into the suffering and grief of victims and their loved ones.

In their statements and actions, each side demonstrates a perspective that fails to recognize any truth in the perspective of the other.

The Palestinian Perspective: For the Palestinian side, "Madrid" and "Oslo" heralded the prospect of a State, and guaranteed an end to the occupation and a resolution of outstanding matters within an agreed time frame.

Palestinians are genuinely angry at the continued growth of settlements and at their daily experiences of humiliation and disruption as a result of Israel's presence in the Palestinian territories. Palestinians see settlers and settlements in their midst not only as violating the spirit of the Oslo process, but also as an application of force in the form of Israel's overwhelming military superiority, which sustains and protects the settlements.

The Interim Agreement provides that "the two parties view the West Bank and Gaza as a single territorial unit, the integrity and status of which will be preserved during the interim period." Coupled with this, the Interim Agreement's prohibition on taking steps which may prejudice permanent status negotiations denies Israel the right to continue its illegal expansionist settlement policy. In addition to the Interim Agreement, customary international law, including the Fourth Geneva Convention, prohibits Israel (as an occupying power) from establishing settlements in occupied territory pending an end to the conflict.[17]

The PLO alleges that Israeli political leaders "have made no secret of the fact that the Israeli interpretation of Oslo was designed to segregate the Palestinians in non-contiguous enclaves, surrounded by Israeli military-controlled borders, with settlements and settlement roads violating the territories' integrity."[18] According to the PLO, "In the seven years since the (Declaration of Principles], the settler population in the West Bank, excluding East Jerusalem and the Gaza Strip, has doubled to 200,000, and the settler population in East Jerusalem has risen to 170,000. Israel has constructed approximately 30 new settlements, and expanded a number of existing ones to house these new settlers."[19]

The PLO also claims that the GOI has failed to comply with other commitments such as the further withdrawal from the West Bank and the release of Palestinian prisoners. In addition, Palestinians expressed frustration with the impasse over refugees and the deteriorating economic circumstances in the West Bank and Gaza Strip.

The Israeli Perspective: From the GOI perspective, the expansion of settlement activity and the taking of measures to facilitate the convenience and safety of settlers do not prejudice the outcome of permanent status negotiations.

Israel understands that the Palestinian side objects to the settlements in the West Bank and the Gaza Strip. Without prejudice to the formal status of the settlements, Israel accepts that the settlements are an outstanding issue on which there will have to be agreement as part of any permanent status resolution between the sides. This point was acknowledged and agreed upon in the Declaration of Principles of 13 September 1993 as well as mother agreements between the two sides. There has in fact been a good deal of discussion on the question of settlements between the two sides in the various negotiations toward a permanent status agreement.[20] Indeed, Israelis point out that at the Camp David summit and during subsequent talks the GOI offered to make significant concessions with respect to settlements in the context of an overall agreement.

Security, however, is the key GOI concern. The GOI maintains that the PLO has breached its solemn commitments by continuing the use of violence in the pursuit of political objectives. "Israel's principal concern in the peace process has been security. This issue is of overriding importance.

[S]ecurity is not something on which Israel will bargain or compromise. The failure of the Palestinian side to comply with both the letter and spirit of the security provisions in the various agreements has long been a source of disturbance in Israel."[21] According to the GOL, the Palestinian failure takes several forms: institutionalized anti-Israel. anti-Jewish incitement; the release from detention of terrorists; the failure to control illegal weapons; and the actual conduct of violent operations, ranging from the insertion of riflemen into demonstrations to terrorist attacks on Israeli civilians. The GOI maintains that the PLO has explicitly violated its renunciation of terrorism and other acts of violence,[22] thereby significantly eroding trust between the parties. The GOI perceives "a thread, implied but nonetheless clear, that runs throughout the Palestinian submissions. It is that Palestinian violence against Israel and Israelis is somehow explicable, understandable, legitimate."[23]

END THE VIOLENCE

For Israelis and Palestinians alike the experience of the past several months has been intensely personal. Through relationships of kinship, friendship, religion, community and profession, virtually everyone in both societies has a link to someone who has been killed or seriously injured in the recent violence. We were touched by their stories.

During our last visit to the region, we met with the families of Palestinian and Israeli victims.

These individual accounts of grief were heart-rending and indescribably sad.

Israeli and Palestinian families used virtually the same words to describe their grief.

When the widow of a murdered Israeli physician—a man of peace whose practice included the treatment of Arab patients—tells us that it seems that Palestinians are interested in killing Jews for the sake of killing Jews, Palestinians should take notice.

When the parents of a Palestinian child killed while in his bed by an errant .50 caliber bullet draw similar conclusions about the respect accorded by Israelis to Palestinian lives, Israelis need to listen. When we see the shattered bodies of children we know it is time for adults to stop the violence.

With widespread violence, both sides have resorted to portrayals of the other in hostile stereotypes. This cycle cannot be easily broken. Without considerable determination and readiness to compromise, the rebuilding of trust will be impossible.

Cessation of Violence: Since 1991, the parties have consistently committed themselves, in all their agreements, to the path of nonviolence. They did so most recently in the two Sharm el-Sheikh summits of September 1999 and October 2000. To stop the violence now, the PA and GOI need not "reinvent the wheel." Rather, they should take immediate steps to end the violence, reaffirm their mutual commitments, and resume negotiations.

Resumption of Security Cooperation: Palestinian security officials told us that it would take some time—perhaps several weeks—for the PA to reassert full control over armed elements nominally under its command and to exert decisive influence over other armed elements operating in Palestinian areas. Israeli security officials have not disputed these assertions. What is important is that the PA make an all-out effort to enforce a complete cessation of violence and that it be clearly seen by the GOI as doing so.

The GOI must likewise exercise a 100 percent effort to ensure that potential friction points, where Palestinians come into contact with armed Israelis do not become stages for renewed hostilities.

The collapse of security cooperation in early October reflected the belief by each party that the other had committed itself to a violent course of action. If the parties wish to attain the standard of 100 percent effort to prevent violence, the immediate resumption of security cooperation is mandatory.

We acknowledge the reluctance of the PA to be seen as facilitating the work of Israeli security services absent an explicit political context (i.e., meaningful negotiations) and under the threat of Israeli settlement expansion. Indeed, security cooperation cannot be sustained without such negotiations and with ongoing actions seen as prejudicing the outcome of negotiations. However, violence is much more likely to continue without security cooperation. Moreover, without effective security cooperation, the parties will continue to regard all acts of violence as officially sanctioned.

In order to overcome the current deadlock, the parties should consider how best to revitalize security cooperation. We commend current efforts to that end. Effective cooperation depends on recreating and sustaining an atmosphere of confidence and good personal relations.

It is for the parties themselves to undertake the main burden of day-to-day cooperation, but they should remain open to engaging the assistance of others in facilitating that work. Such outside assistance should be by mutual consent, should not threaten good bilateral working arrangements, and should not act as a tribunal or interpose between the parties. There was good security cooperation until last year that benefitted from the good offices of the U.S. (acknowledged by both sides as useful), and was also supported indirectly by security projects and assistance from the European Union. The role of outside assistance should be that of creating the appropriate framework, sustaining goodwill on both sides, and removing friction where possible. That framework must be seen to be contributing to the safety and welfare of both communities if there is to be acceptance by those communities of these efforts.

REBUILD CONFIDENCE

The historic handshake between Chairman Arafat and the late Prime Minister Rabin at the White House in September 1993 symbolized the expectation of both parties that the door to the peaceful resolution of differences had been opened. Despite the current violence and mutual loss of trust, both communities have repeatedly expressed a desire for peace. Channeling this desire into substantive progress has proved difficult. The restoration of trust is essential, and the parties should take affirmative steps to this end. Given the high level of hostility and mistrust, the timing and sequence of these steps are obviously crucial. This can be decided only by the parties. We urge them to begin the process of decision immediately.

Terrorism: In the September 1999 Sharm el-Sheikh Memorandum, the parties pledged to take action against "any threat or act of terrorism, violence or incitement." Although all three categories of hostilities are reprehensible, it was no accident that "terrorism" was placed at the top of the list.

Terrorism involves the deliberate killing and injuring of randomly selected noncombatants for political ends. It seeks to promote a political outcome by spreading terror and demoralization throughout a population. It is immoral and ultimately self defeating. We condemn it and we urge that the parties coordinate their security efforts to eliminate it.

In its official submissions and briefings, the GOI has accused the PA of supporting terrorism by releasing incarcerated terrorists, by allowing PA security personnel to abet, and in some cases to conduct terrorist operations, and by terminating security cooperation with the GOI. The PA vigorously denies the accusations. But Israelis hold the view that the PA's leadership has made no real effort over the past seven months to prevent anti-Israeli terrorism. The belief is, in and of itself, a major obstacle to the rebuilding of confidence.

We believe that the PA has a responsibility to help rebuild confidence by making clear to both communities that terrorism is reprehensible and unacceptable, and by taking all measures to prevent terrorist operations and to punish perpetrators. This effort should include immediate steps to apprehend and incarcerate terrorists operating within the PA's jurisdiction.

Settlements: The GOI also has a responsibility to help rebuild confidence. A cessation of Palestinian-Israeli violence will be particularly hard to sustain unless the GOI freezes all settlement construction activity. The GOI should also give careful consideration to whether settlements that are focal points for substantial friction are valuable bargaining chips for future negotiations or provocations likely to preclude the onset of productive talks.

The issue is, of course, controversial. Many Israelis will regard our recommendation as a statement of the obvious, and will support it. Many will oppose it. But settlement activities must not be allowed to undermine the restoration of calm and the resumption of negotiations.

During the half-century of its existence, Israel has had the strong support of the United States. In international forums, the US. has at times cast the only vote on Israel's behalf. Yet, even in such a close relationship there are some differences.

Prominent among those differences is the U.S. Government's long-standing opposition to the GOI's policies and practices regarding settlements. As the then-Secretary of State, James A.

Baker, III, commented on May 22, 1991: Every time I have gone to Israel in connection with the peace process, on each of my four trips, I have been met with the announcement of new settlement activity. This does violate United States policy. It's the first thing that Arabs—Arab Governments, the first thing that the Palestinians in the territories—whose situation is really quite desperate—the first thing they raise when we talk to them. I don't think there is any bigger obstacle to peace than the settlement activity that continues not only unabated but at an enhanced pace.[24] The policy described by Secretary Baker, on behalf of the Administration of President George H. W. Bush. has been, in essence, the policy of every American administration over the past quarter century.[25]

Most other countries, including Turkey, Norway, and those of the European Union, have also been critical of Israeli settlement activity, in accordance with their views that such settlements are illegal under international law and not in compliance with previous agreements.

On each of our two visits to the region there were Israeli announcements regarding expansion of settlements, and it was almost always the first issue raised by Palestinians with whom we met. During our last visit, we observed the impact of 6,400 settlers on 140,000 Palestinians in Hebron [26] and 6,500 settlers on over 1,100,000 Palestinians in the Gaza Strip.[27] The GOI describes its policy as prohibiting new settlements but permitting expansion of existing settlements to accommodate "natural growth." Palestinians contend that there is no distinction between new' and "expanded" settlements; and that, except for a brief freeze during the tenure of Prime Minister Yitzak Rabin, there has been a continuing, aggressive effort by Israel to increase the number and size of settlements.

The subject has been widely discussed within Israel. The Ha'aretz English Language Edition editorial of April 10, 2001 stated: A government which seeks to argue that its goal is to reach a solution to the conflict with the Palestinians through peaceful means, and is trying at this stage to bring an end to the violence and terrorism, must announce an end to construction in the settlements.[28]

The circumstances in the region are much changed from those which existed nearly 20 years ago. Yet, President Reagan's words remain relevant: "The immediate adoption of a settlements freeze by Israel, more than any other action, could create the confidence needed Beyond the obvious confidence-building qualities of a settlement freeze, we note that many of the confrontations during this conflict have occurred at points where Palestinians, settlers, and security forces protecting the settlers, meet. Keeping both the peace and these friction points will be very difficult.

Reducing Tension: We were told by both Palestinians and Israelis that emotions generated by the many recent deaths and funerals have fueled additional confrontations, and. in effect, maintained the cycle of violence.

We cannot urge one side or the other to refrain from demonstrations. But both sides must make clear that violent demonstrations will not be tolerated. We can and do urge that both sides exhibit a greater respect for human life when demonstrators confront security personnel. In addition, a renewed effort to stop the violence might feature, for a limited time, a "cooling off" period during which public demonstrations at or near friction points will be discouraged in order to break the cycle of violence. To the extent that demonstrations. continue, we urge that demonstrators and security personnel keep their distance from one another to reduce the potential for lethal confrontation.

Actions and Responses: Members of the Committee staff witnessed an incident involving stone throwing in Ramallah from the perspectives, on the ground, of both sides. The people confronting one another were mostly young men. The absence of senior leadership on the IDF side was striking. Likewise, the absence of responsible security and other officials counseling restraint on the Palestinian side was obvious.

Concerning such confrontations, the GOI takes the position that "Israel is engaged in an armed conflict short of war. This is not a civilian disturbance or a demonstration or a riot. It is characterized by live-fire attacks on a significant scale [emphasis added]…The attacks are carried out by a well-armed and organized militia…"[29] Yet, the GOI acknowledges that of some 9,000 "attacks" by Palestinians against Israelis, "some 2,700 [about 30 percent] involved the use of automatic weapons, rifles, hand guns, grenades, [and] explosives of other kinds."[30] Thus, for the first three months of the current uprising, most incidents did not involve Palestinian use of firearms and explosives. B'Tselem reported that, "according to IDF figures, 73 percent of the incidents [from September 29 to December 2, 2000] did not include Palestinian gunfire.

Despite this, it was in these incidents that most of the Palestinians [were] killed and wounded…"[31] Altogether, nearly 500 people were killed and over 10,000 injured over the past seven months; the overwhelming majority in both categories were Palestinian.

Many of these deaths were avoidable, as were many Israeli deaths.

Israel's characterization of the conflict, as noted above, is overly broad, for it does not adequately describe the variety of incidents reported since late September 2000.

Moreover, by thus defining the conflict, the IDF has suspended its policy of mandating investigations by the Department of Military Police Investigations whenever a Palestinian in the territories dies at the hands of an IDF soldier in an incident not involving terrorism.

In the words of the GOI, "Where Israel considers that there is reason to investigate particular incidents, it does so, although, given the circumstances of armed conflict, it does not do so routinely."[32] We believe, however, that by abandoning the blanket "armed conflict short of war" characterization and by re-instituting mandatory military police investigations, the GOI could help mitigate deadly violence and help rebuild mutual confidence. Notwithstanding the danger posed by stone-throwers, an effort should be made to differentiate between terrorism and protests.

Controversy has arisen between the parties over what Israel calls the "targeting of individual enemy combatants."[33] The PLO describes these actions as "extra-judicial executions,"[34] and claims that Israel has engaged in an "assassination policy" that is "in clear violation of Article 32 of the Fourth Geneva Convention…"[35] The GOI states that, "whatever action Israel has taken has been taken firmly within the bounds of the relevant and accepted principles relating to the conduct of hostilities."[36] With respect to demonstrations, the GOI has acknowledged "that individual instances of excessive response may have occurred. To a soldier or a unit coming under Palestinian attack, the equation is not that of the Israeli army versus some stone throwing Palestinian protesters. It is a personal equation."[37] We understand this concern, particularly since rocks can maim or even kill.

It is no easy matter for a few young soldiers, confronted by large numbers of hostile demonstrators, to make fine legal distinctions on the spot.

Still, this "personal equation" must fit within an organizational ethic; in this case, "The Ethical Code of the Israel Defense Forces, which states, in part: The sanctity of human life in the eyes of the IDF servicemen will find expression in all of their actions, in deliberate and meticulous planning, in safe and intelligent training and in proper execution of their mission.

In evaluating the risk to self and others, they will use the appropriate standards and will exercise constant care to limit injury to life to the extent required to accomplish the mission.[38] Those required to respect the IDF ethical code are largely draftees, as the IDF is a conscript force. Active duty enlisted personnel, noncommissioned officers and junior officers—the categories most likely to be present at friction points—are young, often teenagers. Unless more senior career personnel or reservists are stationed at friction points, no IDF personnel present in these sensitive areas have experience to draw upon from previous violent Israeli-Palestinian confrontations. We think it is essential, especially in the context of restoring confidence by minimizing deadly confrontations, that the IDF deploy more senior, experienced soldiers to these sensitive points.

There were incidents where IDF soldiers have used lethal force, including live ammunition and modified metal-cored rubber rounds, against unarmed demonstrators throwing stones. [39] The IDF should adopt crowd-control tactics that minimize the potential for deaths and casualties, withdrawing metal-cored rubber rounds from general use and using instead rubber baton rounds without metal cores.

We are deeply concerned about the public safety implications of exchanges of fire between populated areas, in particular between Israeli settlements and neighboring Palestinian villages. Palestinian gunmen have directed small arms fire at Israeli settlements and at nearby IDF positions from within or adjacent to civilian dwellings in Palestinian areas, thus endangering innocent Israeli. and Palestinian civilians alike. We condemn the positioning of gunmen within or near civilian dwellings. The TIDF often responds to such gunfire with heavy caliber weapons, sometimes resulting in deaths and injuries to innocent Palestinians. An IDF officer told us at the Ministry of Defense on March 23, 2001 that, "When shooting comes from a building we respond, and sometimes there are innocent people in the building." Obviously, innocent people are injured and killed during exchanges of this nature. We urge that such provocations cease and that the IDF exercise maximum restraint in its responses if they do occur.

Inappropriate or excessive uses of force often lead to escalation.

We are aware of IDF sensitivities about these subjects. More than once we were asked: "What about Palestinian rules of engagement? What about a Palestinian code of ethics for their military personnel?" These are valid questions.

On the Palestinian side there are disturbing ambiguities in the basic areas of responsibility and accountability. The lack of control exercised by the PA over its own security personnel and armed elements affiliated with the PA leadership is very troubling. We urge the PA to take all necessary steps to establish a clear and unchallenged chain of command for armed personnel operating under its authority. We recommend that the PA institute and enforce effective standards of conduct and accountability, both within the uniformed ranks and between the police and the civilian political leadership to which it reports.

Incitement: In their submissions and briefings to the Committee, both sides expressed concerns about hateful language and images emanating from the other, citing numerous examples of hostile sectarian and ethnic rhetoric in the Palestinian and Israeli media, in school curricula and in statements by religious leaders, politicians and others.

We call on the parties to renew their formal commitments to foster mutual understanding and tolerance and to abstain from incitement and hostile propaganda. We condemn hate language and incitement in all its forms. We suggest that the parties be particularly cautious about using words in a manner that suggests collective responsibility.

Economic and Social Impact of Violence: Further restrictions on the movement of people and goods have been imposed by Israel on the West Bank and the Gaza Strip. These closures take three forms: those which restrict movement between the Palestinian areas and Israel; those (including curfews) which restrict movement within the Palestinian areas; and those which restrict movement from the Palestinian areas to foreign countries. These measures have disrupted the lives of hundreds of thousands of Palestinians; they have increased Palestinian unemployment to an estimated 40 percent. in part by preventing some 140,000 Palestinians from working in Israel; and have stripped away about one-third of the Palestinian gross domestic product.

Moreover, the transfer of tax and customs duty revenues owed to the PA by Israel has been suspended, leading to a serious fiscal crisis in the PA.

Of particular concern to the PA has been the destruction by Israeli security forces and settlers of tens of thousands of olive and fruit trees and other agricultural property. The closures have had other adverse effects, such as preventing civilians from access to urgent medical treatment and preventing students from attending school.

The GOI maintains that these measures were taken in order to protect Israeli citizens from terrorism. Palestinians characterize these measures as "collective punishment." The GOI denies the allegation: Israel has not taken measures that have had an economic impact simply for the sake of taking such measures or for reasons of harming the Palestinian economy. The measures have been taken for reasons of security. Thus, for example. the closure of the Palestinian territories was taken in order to prevent, or at least minimize the risks of, terrorist attacks...The Palestinian leadership has made no attempt to control this activity and bring it to an end.[40]

Moreover, the GOI points out that violence in the last quarter of 2000 cost the Israeli economy $1.2 billion (USD), and that the loss continues at a rate of approximately $150 million (USD) per month.[41] We acknowledge Israel's security concerns. We believe, however, that the GOI should lift closures, transfer to the PA all revenues owed, and permit Palestinians who have been employed in Israel to return to their jobs.

Closure policies play into the hands of extremists seeking to expand their constituencies and thereby contribute to escalation. The PA should resume cooperation with Israeli security agencies to ensure that Palestinian workers employed within Israel are fully vetted and free of connections to terrorists and terrorist organizations.

International development assistance has from the start been an integral part of the peace process, with an aim to strengthen the socio-economic foundations for peace. This assistance today is more important than ever. We urge the international community to sustain the development agenda of the peace process.

Holy Places: It is particularly regrettable that places such as the Temple Mount/Haram al-Sharif in Jerusalem, Joseph's Tomb in Nablus, and Rachel's Tomb in Bethlehem have been the scenes of violence, death and injury. These are places of peace, prayer and reflection which must be accessible to all believers.

Places deemed holy by Muslims, Jews, and Christians merit respect, protection and preservation. Agreements previously reached by the parties regarding holy places must be upheld. The GOI and the PA should create a joint initiative to defuse the sectarian aspect of their political dispute by preserving and protecting such places. Efforts to develop inter-faith dialogue should be encouraged.

International Force: One of the most controversial subjects raised during our inquiry was the issue of deploying an international force to the Palestinian areas. The PA is strongly in favor of having such a force to protect Palestinian civilians and their property from the IDF and from settlers. The GOI is just as adamantly opposed to an "international protection force," believing that it would prove unresponsive to Israeli security concerns and interfere with bilateral negotiations to settle the conflict.

We believe that to be effective such a force would need the support of both parties.

We note that international forces deployed in this region have been or are in a position to fulfill their mandates and make a positive contribution only when they were deployed with the consent of all of the parties involved.

During our visit to Hebron we were briefed by personnel of the Temporary International Presence in Hebron (TIPH), a presence to which both parties have agreed. The TIPH is charged with observing an explosive situation and writing reports on their observations.

If the parties agree, as a confidence-building measure, to draw upon TIPH personnel to help them manage other friction points, we hope that TIPH contributors could accommodate such a request.

Cross-Community Initiatives: Many described to us the near absolute loss of trust. It was all the more inspiring, therefore, to find groups (such as the Parent's Circle and the Economic Cooperation Foundation) dedicated to cross-community understanding in spite of all that has happened. We commend them and their important work.

Regrettably, most of the work of this nature has stopped during the current conflict.

To help rebuild confidence, the GOI and PA should jointly endorse and support the work of Israeli and Palestinian non-governmental organizations (NGOs) already involved in confidence building through initiatives linking both sides. It is important that the PA and GOI support cross-community organizations and initiatives, including the provision of humanitarian assistance to Palestinian villages by Israeli NGOs. Providing travel permits for participants is essential. Cooperation between the humanitarian organizations and the military/security services of the parties should be encouraged and institutionalized.

Such programs can help build, albeit slowly, constituencies for peace among Palestinians and Israelis and can provide safety nets during times of turbulence.

Organizations involved in this work are vital for translating good intentions into positive actions.

RESUME NEGOTIATIONS

Israeli leaders do not wish to be perceived as "rewarding violence." Palestinian leaders do not wish to be perceived as "rewarding occupation." We appreciate the political constraints on leaders of both sides.

Nevertheless, if the cycle of violence is to be broken and the search for peace resumed, there needs to be a new bilateral relationship incorporating both security cooperation and negotiations.

We cannot prescribe to the parties how best to pursue their political objectives. Yet the construction of a new bilateral relationship solidifying and transcending an agreed cessation of violence requires intelligent risk-taking. It requires, in the first instance, that each party again be willing to regard the other as a partner. Partnership, in turn, requires at this juncture something more than was agreed in the Declaration of Principles and in subsequent agreements. Instead of declaring the peace process to be "dead," the parties should determine how they will conclude their common journey along their agreed "road map!' a journey which began in Madrid and continued in spite of problems—until very recently.

To define a starting point is for the parties to decide. Both parties have stated that they remain committed to their mutual agreements and undertakings. It is time to explore further implementation. The parties should declare their intention to meet on this basis, in order to resume full and meaningful negotiations, in the spirit of their undertakings at Sharm el-Sheikh in 1999 and 2000.

Neither side will be able to achieve its principal objectives unilaterally or without political risk. We know how hard it is for leaders to act—especially if the action can be characterized by political opponents as a concession—without getting something in return. The PA must—as it has at previous critical junctures take steps to reassure Israel on security matters. The GOI must—as it has in the past—take steps to reassure the PA on political matters. Israelis and Palestinians should avoid, in their own actions and attitudes, giving extremists, common criminals and revenge seekers the final say in defining their joint future. This will not be easy if deadly incidents occur in spite of effective cooperation. Notwithstanding the daunting difficulties, the very foundation of the trust required to reestablish a functioning partnership consists of each side making such strategic reassurances to the other.

RECOMMENDATIONS

The GOI and the PA must act swiftly and decisively to halt the violence.

Their immediate objectives then should be to rebuild confidence and resume negotiations. What we are asking is not easy. Palestinians and Israelis—not just their leaders, but two publics at large—have lost confidence in one another. We are asking political leaders to do, for the sake of their people, the politically difficult: to lead without knowing how many will follow.

During this mission our aim has been to fulfill the mandate agreed at Sharm el-Sheikh.

We value the support given our work by the participants at the summit, and we commend the parties for their cooperation. Our principal recommendation is that they recommit themselves to the Sharm el-Sheikh spirit, and that they implement the decisions made there in 1999 and 2000.

We believe that the summit participants will support bold action by the parties to achieve these objectives.

END THE VIOLENCE

- The GOI and the PA should reaffirm their commitment to existing agreements and undertakings and should immediately implement an unconditional cessation of violence.
  Anything less than a complete effort by both parties to end the violence will render the effort itself ineffective, and will likely be interpreted by the other side as evidence of hostile intent.

- The GOI and PA should immediately resume security cooperation.
  Effective bilateral cooperation aimed at preventing violence will encourage the resumption of negotiations. We are particularly concerned that, absent effective, transparent security cooperation, terrorism and other acts of violence will continue and may be seen as officially sanctioned whether they are or not. The parties should consider widening the scope of security cooperation to reflect the priorities of both communities and to seek acceptance for these efforts from those communities.
  We acknowledge the PA's position that security cooperation presents a political difficulty absent a suitable political context, i.e., the relaxation of stringent Israeli security measures combined with ongoing, fruitful negotiations. We also acknowledge the PA's fear that, with security cooperation in hand., the GOI may not be disposed to deal forthrightly with Palestinian political concerns. We believe that security cooperation cannot long be sustained if meaningful negotiations are unreasonably deferred, if security measures "on the ground" are seen as hostile, or if steps are taken that are perceived as provocative or as prejudicing the outcome of negotiations.

REBUILD CONFIDENCE

- The PA and GOI should work together to establish a meaningful "cooling off period" and implement additional confidence building measures, some of which were proposed in the October 2000 Sharm el-Sheikh Statement and some of which were offered by the U.S. on January 7, 2001 in Cairo.

- The PA and GOI should resume their efforts to identify, condemn and discourage incitement in all its forms.

- The PA should make clear through concrete action to Palestinians and Israelis alike that terrorism is reprehensible and unacceptable, and that the PA will make a 100 percent effort to prevent terrorist operations and to punish perpetrators. This effort should include immediate steps to apprehend and incarcerate terrorists operating within the PA's jurisdiction.

- The GOI should freeze all settlement activity, including the "natural growth" of existing settlements.
  The kind of security cooperation desired by the GOI cannot for long co-exist with settlement activity described very recently by the European Union as causing "great concern" and by the U.S. as "provocative." * The GOI should give careful consideration to whether settlements which are focal points for substantial friction are valuable bargaining chips for future negotiations or provocations likely to preclude the onset of productive talks.

- The GOI may wish to make it clear to the PA that a future peace would pose no threat to the territorial contiguity of a Palestinian State to be established in the West Bank and the Gaza Strip.

- The IDF should consider withdrawing to positions held before September 28, 2000 which will reduce the number of friction points and the potential for violent confrontations.

- The GOI should ensure that the IDF adopt and enforce policies and procedures encouraging non-lethal responses to unarmed demonstrators, with a view to minimizing casualties and friction between the two communities. The IDF should: * Re-institute, as a matter of course, military police investigations into Palestinian deaths resulting from IDF actions in the Palestinian territories in incidents not involving terrorism. The IDF should abandon the blanket characterization of the current uprising as "an armed conflict short of war," which fails to discriminate between terrorism and protest.

- Adopt tactics of crowd-control that minimize the potential for deaths and casualties, including the withdrawal of metal-cored rubber rounds from general use.

- Ensure that experienced, seasoned personnel are present for duty at all times at known friction points.

- Ensure that the stated values and standard operating procedures of the IDF effectively instill the duty of caring for Palestinians in the West Bank and Gaza Strip as well as Israelis living there, consistent with The Ethical Code of The IDF.

- The GOI should lift closures, transfer to the PA all tax revenues owed, and permit Palestinians who had been employed in Israel to return to their jobs; and should ensure that security forces and settlers refrain from the destruction of homes and roads, as well as trees and other agricultural property in Palestinian areas. We acknowledge the GOI's position that actions of this nature have been taken for security reasons. Nevertheless, their economic effects will persist for years.

- The PA should renew cooperation with Israeli security agencies to ensure, to the maximum extent possible, that Palestinian workers employed within Israel are fully vetted and free of connections to organizations and individuals engaged in terrorism.

- The PA should prevent gunmen from using Palestinian populated areas to fire upon Israeli populated areas and IDF positions. This tactic places civilians on both sides at unnecessary risk.

- The GOI and IDF should adopt and enforce policies and procedures designed to ensure that the response to any gunfire emanating from Palestinian populated areas minimizes the danger to the lives and property of Palestinian civilians, bearing in mind that it is probably the objective of gunmen to elicit an excessive IDF response.

- The GOI should take all necessary steps to prevent acts of violence by settlers.

- The parties should abide by the provisions of the Wye River Agreement prohibiting illegal weapons.

- The PA should take all necessary steps to establish a clear and unchallenged chain of command for armed personnel operating under its authority.

- The PA should institute and enforce effective standards of conduct and accountability, both within the uniformed ranks and between the police and the civilian political leadership to which it reports.

- The PA and GOI should consider a joint undertaking to preserve and protect holy places sacred to the traditions of Muslims, Jews, and Christians. An initiative of this nature might help to reverse a disturbing trend: the increasing use of religious themes to encourage and justify violence.

- The GOI and PA should jointly endorse and support the work of Palestinian and Israeli non-governmental organizations (NGOs) involved in cross-community initiatives linking the two peoples. It is important that these activities, including the provision of humanitarian aid to Palestinian villages by Israeli NGOs, receive the full backing of both parties.

RESUME NEGOTIATIONS

- We reiterate our belief that a 100 percent effort to stop the violence, an immediate resumption of security cooperation and an exchange of confidence building measures are all important for the resumption of negotiations. Yet none of these steps will long be sustained absent a return to serious negotiations.
It is not within our mandate to prescribe the venue, the basis or the agenda of negotiations. However, in order to provide an effective political context for practical cooperation between the parties, negotiations must not be unreasonably deferred and they must, in our view, manifest a spirit of compromise, reconciliation and partnership, notwithstanding the events of the past seven months.

- In the spirit of the Sharm el-Sheikh agreements and understandings of 1999 and 2000, we recommend that the parties meet to reaffirm their commitment to signed agreements and mutual understandings, and take corresponding action.
This should be the basis for resuming full and meaningful negotiations.
The parties are at a crossroads. If they do not return to the negotiating table, they face the prospect of fighting it out for years on end, with many of their citizens leaving for distant shores to live their lives and raise their children. We pray they make the right choice. That means stopping the violence now. Israelis and Palestinians have to live, work, and prosper together. History and geography have destined them to be neighbors. That cannot be changed. Only when their actions are guided by this awareness will they be able to develop the vision and reality of peace and shared prosperity.
Suleyman Demirel 9th President of the Republic of Turkey Thorbjoern Jagland Minister of Foreign Affairs of Norway George J. Mitchell, Chairman Former Member and Majority Leader of the United States Senate Warren B. Rudman Former Member of the United States Senate Javier Solana High Representative for the Common Foreign and Security Policy, European Union

FOOTNOTES

1. A copy of the statement is attached.

2. Copies of the President's letters are attached.

3. When informed of the planned visit, Ambassador Dennis Ross (President Clinton's Middle East Envoy) said that he told Israeli Minister of Interior Shlomo Ben-Ami, "I can think of a lot of bad ideas, but I can't think of a worse one." See Jane Perlez, "US Envoy Recalls the Day Pandora's Box Wouldn' t Shut," The New York Times, January 29, 2001.

4. U.S. Department of State, Country Reports on Human Rights Practices—2000 (Israel), Bureau of Democracy, Human Rights and Labor, February 2001, http://www.state.gov/g/drl/rlsi/hrrpt/2000/nea/index.

5. Government of Israel, First Statement. 28 December 2000 (hereafter "GOI. First Statement"), 187. B'Tselem (The Israeli Information Center for Human Rights in the Occupied Territories) reported that 70 police were injured. See Events on the Temple Mount—29 September 2000: Interim Report, http://www.btselem.org/files/site/Violent Events/Temple-Mount-2000 eng.as

6. Disturbances also occurred within Israel's Arab community, resulting in thirteen deaths. These events do not fall within the mandate of this Committee and are the subject of an official GOI inquiry.

7. GOI. First Statement, 118.

8. Id., 110. According to the GOI, the Palestinian Minister of Posts and Telecommunications declared at a rally in Lebanon in March 2001 that the confrontation with Israel had been planned following the Camp David Summit. See Government of Israel, Second Statement, 20 March 2001 (hereafter, "GOI, Second Statement"), 2. The PA provided the Committee a translation of a letter from the Minister, dated March 12. 2001. in which the Minister denied saying that the intifada was planned, and that his statement in Lebanon was misquoted and taken out of context. We were told by an Israeli Defense Force (IDF) intelligence officer that while the declaration itself was not definitive, it represented an "open-source" version of what was known to

the IDF through "other means"; knowledge and means not shared by the IDF with the Committee.

9. Palestine Liberation Organization. Preliminary Submission of the Palestine Liberation Organization to the International Commission of Inquiry, December 8, 2000, p.

10. Note: submissions to the Committee from the Palestinian side were made by the PLO./
    10 Palestine Liberation Organization. A Crisis of Faith: Second Submission 0/the Palestine Liberation Organization to the Sharm El-Sheikh Fact-Finding Committee, December 30, 2000 (hereafter "PLO, Second Submission"), p. 16.

11. See GOI, First Statement. 286.

12. Palestine Liberation Organization, Third Submission of the Palestine Liberation Organization to the Sharm El-Sheikh Fact-Finding Committee, April 3, 2001 (hereafter "PLO, Third Submission"), p. 51.

13. GOI. Second Statement, 4.

14. GOI, First Statement, 19.

15. PLO, Third Submission, p. 25.

16. Id., pp. 46-50.

17. Id., pp. 27-28 18 PLO, Second Submission, p. 14.

18. Id., pp. 14-15.

19. GOI. Second Statement, 82.

20. GOI, First Statement, 99.

21. GOI, Second Statement, 19, referring to the Exchange of Notes Between the Prime Minister of Israel and the Chairman of the PLO, 9-10 September 1993.

22. Id.,21.

23. Testimony before the United States House of Representatives Committee on Appropriations, 102nd Congress, May 22. 1991.

24. On March 21, 1980, Secretary of State Cyrus Vance, speaking on behalf of the Carter Administration, stated: "U.S. policy toward the establishment of Israeli settlements in the occupied territories is unequivocal and has long been a matter of public record. We consider it to be contrary to international law and an impediment to the successful conclusion of the Middle East peace process." On September 1, 1982, President Ronald Reagan announced what came to be known as The Reagan Plan for the Middle East, stating that: "[T]he immediate adoption of a settlements freeze by Israel, more than any other action, could create the confidence needed for wider participation in these talks.
Further settlement activity is in no way necessary for the security of Israel and only diminishes the confidence of the Arabs that a final outcome can be freely and fairly negotiated." On December 16, 1996, at a press conference. President Bill Clinton stated: "It just stands to reason that anything that pre-empts the outcome [of the negotiations]...cannot be helpful in making peace. I don't think anything should be done that would be seen as preempt-ing the outcome." Asked if he viewed the settlements as an obstacle to peace, President Clinton replied, "Absolutely. Absolutely." On April 5, 2001, a U.S. State Department spokesman, speaking for the current administration, stated: "Continuing settlement activity does risk inflaming an already vola-tile situation in the region"; he described that activity as "provocative."

25. There are 400 settlers in the "H2" sector of central Hebron. and 6.000 in the Kiryat Arba settlement on the eastern edge of the city. See "An Introduction to the City of Hebron," published by the Temporary International Presence in Hebron, http://www.tiph.org

26. Central Intelligence Agency. The World Factbook 2000, http://www.cia.gov/cia/publications/factbook/geos/gz.html

27. Ha'aretz, English Language Edition, April 10. 2001, p. 5.

28. GOI, First Statement, 286.

29. Id., 189.

30. B'Tselem, Illusions of Restraint. Human Rig/its Violations During the Events in the Occupied Territories, 29 September-2 December 2000, December 2000, p. 4.

31. GOI First Statement, 306. "The stated policy of the IDF is that whenever a Palestinian in the Occupied Territories dies at the hands of a soldier, an investigation is to be made by the Department of Military Police Investigations (MPI), except in cases defined as 'hostile terrorist activity'." See B'Tselem, Illusions of Restraint, p. 24.
    See also, Alex Fishman, "The Intifada, the IDF and Investigations," Yediot Aharonot (in English, Richard Bell Press, 1996, Ltd.), January 19, 2001.

32. GOI, Second Statement. 69-80.

33. PLO, Third Submission, p. 69.

34. Id., p. 60.

35. GOI, Second Statement, 78.

36. GOI. First Statement, 305.

37. Israel Defense Forces, The Ethical Code of the Israel Defense Forces.
    http://www.idf.il/english/doctrine/doctrine.stm

38. See, e.g., U.S. Department of State, Country Reports on Human Rights Practices, 2000 (Occupied Territories), http://www.state.gov/g/drl/rls/hrrpt/2000/nea/index. See also, B'Tselem, Illusions of Restraint, pp. 15-16, reporting on the alleged practice of separating rubber bullets into individual rounds, as opposed to firing them properly in a bound cluster of three. Separation increases range and lethality.

39. GOI, Second Statement, 92.

40. Id., 89.
    Last revised on 22 May, 2001

APPENDIX C

United Nations Resolutions 242 and 338 Upon Which The Oslo Agreements Were Based

U.N. SECURITY COUNCIL RESOLUTION 242

November 22, 1967

Following the June '67, Six-Day War, the situation in the Middle East was discussed by the UN General Assembly, which referred the issue to the Security Council. After lengthy discussion, a final draft for a Security Council resolution was presented by the British Ambassador, Lord Caradon, on November 22, 1967. It was adopted on the same day.

This resolution, numbered 242, established provisions and principles which, it was hoped, would lead to a solution of the conflict. Resolution 242 was to become the cornerstone of Middle East diplomatic efforts in the coming decades.

The Security Council,

Expressing its continuing concern with the grave situation in the Middle East,

Emphasizing the inadmissibility of the acquisition of territory by war and the need to work for a just and lasting peace in which every State in the area can live in security,

Emphasizing further that all Member States in their acceptance of the Charter of the United Nations have undertaken a commitment to act in accordance with Article 2 of the Charter,

Affirms that the fulfillment of Charter principles requires the establishment of a just and lasting peace in the Middle East which should include the application of both the following principles:

- Withdrawal of Israeli armed forces from territories occupied in the recent conflict;

- Termination of all claims or states of belligerency and respect for and acknowledgement of the sovereignty, territorial integrity and political independence of every State in the area and their right to live in peace within secure and recognized boundaries free from threats or acts of force;

Affirms further the necessity

- For guaranteeing freedom of navigation through international waterways in the area;

- For achieving a just settlement of the refugee problem;

- For guaranteeing the territorial inviolability and political independence of every State in the area, through measures including the establishment of demilitarized zones;

Requests the Secretary General to designate a Special Representative to proceed to the Middle East to establish and maintain contacts with the States concerned in order to promote agreement and assist efforts to achieve a peaceful and accepted settlement in accordance with the provisions and principles in this resolution;

Requests the Secretary-General to report to the Security Council on the progress of the efforts of the Special Representative as soon as possible.

U.N. SECURITY COUNCIL RESOLUTION 338

October 22, 1973

In the later stages of the Yom Kippur War—after Israel repulsed the Syrian attack on the Golan Heights and established a bridgehead on the Egyptian side of the Suez Canal—international efforts to stop the fighting were intensified. US Secretary of State Kissinger flew to Moscow on October 20, and, together with the Soviet Government, the US proposed a cease-fire resolution in the UN Security Council. The Council met on 21 October at the urgent request of both the US and the USSR, and by 14 votes to none, adopted the following resolution:

The Security Council,

Calls upon all parties to present fighting to cease all firing and terminate all military activity immediately, no later than 12 hours after the moment of the adoption of this decision, in the positions after the moment of the adoption of this decision, in the positions they now occupy;

Calls upon all parties concerned to start immediately after the cease-fire the implementation of Security Council Resolution 242 (1967) in all of its parts;

Decides that, immediately and concurrently with the cease-fire, negotiations start between the parties concerned under appropriate auspices aimed at establishing a just and durable peace in the Middle East.

APPENDIX D

QUARTET PLAN:
Roadmap to a Permanent Two-State Solution to the Israeli-Palestinian Conflict

The following is a performance-based and goal-driven roadmap, with clear phases, timelines, target dates, and benchmarks aiming at progress through reciprocal steps by the two parties in the political, security, economic, humanitarian, and institution-building fields, under the auspices of the Quartet [the United States, European Union, United Nations, and Russia]. The destination is a final and comprehensive settlement of the Israel-Palestinian conflict by 2005, as presented in President Bush's speech of 24 June, and welcomed by the EU, Russia and the UN in the 16 July and 17 September Quartet Ministerial statements.

A two-state solution to the Israeli-Palestinian conflict will only be achieved through an end to violence and terrorism, when the Palestinian people have a leadership acting decisively against terror and willing and able to build a practicing democracy based on tolerance and liberty, and through Israel's readiness to do what is necessary for a democratic Palestinian state to be established, and a clear, unambiguous acceptance by both parties of the goal of a negotiated settlement as described below. The Quartet will assist and facilitate implementation of the plan, starting in Phase I, including direct discussions between the parties as required. The plan establishes a realistic timeline for implementation. However, as a performance-based plan, progress will require and depend upon the good faith efforts of the parties, and their compliance with each of the obligations outlined below. Should the parties perform their obligations rapidly, progress within and through the phases may come sooner than indicated in the plan. Non-compliance with obligations will impede progress.

A settlement, negotiated between the parties, will result in the emergence of an independent, democratic, and viable Palestinian state living side by side in peace and security with Israel and its other neighbors. The settlement will resolve the Israel-Palestinian conflict, and end the occupation that began in 1967, based on the foundations of the Madrid Conference, the principle of land for peace, UNSCRs 242, 338 and 1397, agreements previously reached by the parties, and the initiative of Saudi Crown Prince Abdullah—endorsed by the Beirut Arab League Summit—calling for acceptance of Israel as a neighbor living in peace and security, in the context of a comprehensive settlement. This initiative is a vital element of international efforts to promote a comprehensive peace on all tracks, including the Syrian-Israeli and Lebanese-Israeli tracks.

The Quartet will meet regularly at senior levels to evaluate the parties' performance on implementation of the plan. In each phase, the parties are expected to perform their obligations in parallel, unless otherwise indicated.

Phase I: Ending Terror And Violence, Normalizing Palestinian Life, and Building Palestinian Institutions—Present to May 2003

In Phase I, the Palestinians immediately undertake an unconditional cessation of violence according to the steps outlined below; such action should be accompanied by supportive measures undertaken by Israel. Palestinians and Israelis resume security cooperation based on the Tenet work plan to end violence, terrorism, and incitement through restructured and effective Palestinian security services. Palestinians undertake comprehensive political reform in preparation for statehood, including drafting a Palestinian constitution, and free, fair and open elections upon the basis of those measures. Israel takes all necessary steps to help normalize Palestinian life. Israel withdraws from Palestinian areas occupied from September 28, 2000 and the two sides restore the status quo that existed at that time, as security performance and cooperation progress. Israel also freezes all settlement activity, consistent with the Mitchell report.

At the outset of Phase I:

- Palestinian leadership issues unequivocal statement reiterating Israel's right to exist in peace and security and calling for an immediate and unconditional ceasefire to end armed activity and all acts of violence against Israelis anywhere. All official Palestinian institutions end incitement against Israel.

- Israeli leadership issues unequivocal statement affirming its commitment to the two-state vision of an independent, viable, sovereign Palestinian state living in peace and security alongside Israel, as expressed by President Bush, and calling for an immediate end to violence against Palestinians everywhere. All official Israeli institutions end incitement against Palestinians.

Security

- Palestinians declare an unequivocal end to violence and terrorism and undertake visible efforts on the ground to arrest, disrupt, and restrain individuals and groups conducting and planning violent attacks on Israelis anywhere.

- Rebuilt and refocused Palestinian Authority security apparatus begins sustained, targeted, and effective operations aimed at confronting all those engaged in terror and dismantlement of terrorist capabilities and infrastructure. This includes commencing confiscation of illegal weapons and consolidation of security authority, free of association with terror and corruption.

- GOI takes no actions undermining trust, including deportations, attacks on civilians; confiscation and/or demolition of Palestinian homes and property, as a punitive measure or to facilitate Israeli construction; destruction of Palestinian institutions and infrastructure; and other measures specified in the Tenet work plan.

- Relying on existing mechanisms and on-the-ground resources, Quartet representatives begin informal monitoring and consult with the parties on establishment of a formal monitoring mechanism and its implementation.

- Implementation, as previously agreed, of U.S. rebuilding, training and resumed security cooperation plan in collaboration with outside oversight board (U.S.–Egypt–Jordan). Quartet support for efforts to achieve a lasting, comprehensive cease-fire.

  - All Palestinian security organizations are consolidated into three services reporting to an empowered Interior Minister.

  - Restructured/retrained Palestinian security forces and IDF counterparts progressively resume security cooperation and other undertakings in implementation of the Tenet work plan, including regular senior-level meetings, with the participation of U.S. security officials.

- Arab states cut off public and private funding and all other forms of support for groups supporting and engaging in violence and terror.

- All donors providing budgetary support for the Palestinians channel these funds through the Palestinian Ministry of Finance's Single Treasury Account.

- As comprehensive security performance moves forward, IDF withdraws progressively from areas occupied since September 28, 2000 and the two sides restore the status quo that existed prior to September 28, 2000. Palestinian security forces redeploy to areas vacated by IDF.

Palestinian Institution-Building

- Immediate action on credible process to produce draft constitution for Palestinian statehood. As rapidly as possible, constitutional committee circulates draft Palestinian constitution, based on strong parliamentary democracy and cabinet with empowered prime minister, for public comment/debate. Constitutional committee proposes draft document for submission after elections for approval by appropriate Palestinian institutions.

- Appointment of interim prime minister or cabinet with empowered executive authority/decision-making body.

- GOI fully facilitates travel of Palestinian officials for PLC and Cabinet sessions, internationally supervised security retraining, electoral and other reform activity, and other supportive measures related to the reform efforts.

- Continued appointment of Palestinian ministers empowered to undertake fundamental reform. Completion of further steps to achieve genuine separation of powers, including any necessary Palestinian legal reforms for this purpose.

- Establishment of independent Palestinian election commission. PLC reviews and revises election law.

- Palestinian performance on judicial, administrative, and economic benchmarks, as established by the International Task Force on Palestinian Reform.

- As early as possible, and based upon the above measures and in the context of open debate and transparent candidate selection/electoral campaign based on a free, multi-party process, Palestinians hold free, open, and fair elections.

- GOI facilitates Task Force election assistance, registration of voters, movement of candidates and voting officials. Support for NGOs involved in the election process.

- GOI reopens Palestinian Chamber of Commerce and other closed Palestinian institutions in East Jerusalem based on a commitment that these institutions operate strictly in accordance with prior agreements between the parties.

Humanitarian Response

- Israel takes measures to improve the humanitarian situation. Israel and Palestinians implement in full all recommendations of the Bertini report to improve humanitarian conditions, lifting curfews and easing restrictions on movement of persons and goods, and allowing full, safe, and unfettered access of international and humanitarian personnel.

- AHLC reviews the humanitarian situation and prospects for economic development in the West Bank and Gaza and launches a major donor assistance effort, including to the reform effort.

- GOI and PA continue revenue clearance process and transfer of funds, including arrears, in accordance with agreed, transparent monitoring mechanism.

Civil Society

- Continued donor support, including increased funding through PVOs/NGOs, for people to people programs, private sector development and civil society initiatives.

Settlements

- GOI immediately dismantles settlement outposts erected since March 2001.

- Consistent with the Mitchell Report, GOI freezes all settlement activity (including natural growth of settlements).

Phase II: Transition—June 2003-December 2003

In the second phase, efforts are focused on the option of creating an independent Palestinian state with provisional borders and attributes of sovereignty, based on the new constitution, as a way station to a permanent status settlement. As has been noted, this goal can be achieved when the Palestinian people have a leadership acting decisively against terror, willing and able to build a practicing democracy based on tolerance and liberty. With such a leadership, reformed civil institutions and security structures, the Palestinians will have the active support of the Quartet and the broader international community in establishing an independent, viable, state.

Progress into Phase II will be based upon the consensus judgment of the Quartet of whether conditions are appropriate to proceed, taking into account performance of both parties. Furthering and sustaining efforts to normalize Palestinian lives and build Palestinian institutions, Phase II starts after Palestinian elections and ends with possible creation of an independent Palestinian state with provisional borders in 2003. Its primary goals are continued comprehensive security performance and effective security cooperation, continued normalization of Palestinian life and institution-building, further building on and sustaining of the goals outlined in Phase I, ratification of a democratic Palestinian constitution, formal establishment of office of prime minister, consolidation of political reform, and the creation of a Palestinian state with provisional borders.

- **International Conference:** Convened by the Quartet, in consultation with the parties, immediately after the successful conclusion of Palestinian elections, to support Palestinian economic recovery and launch a process, leading to establishment of an independent Palestinian state with provisional borders.

  - Such a meeting would be inclusive, based on the goal of a comprehensive Middle East peace (including between Israel and Syria, and Israel and Lebanon), and based on the principles described in the preamble to this document.

  - Arab states restore pre-intifada links to Israel (trade offices, etc.).

  - Revival of multilateral engagement on issues including regional water resources, environment, economic development, refugees, and arms control issues.

- New constitution for democratic, independent Palestinian state is finalized and approved by appropriate Palestinian institutions. Further elections, if required, should follow approval of the new constitution.

  - Empowered reform cabinet with office of prime minister formally established, consistent with draft constitution.

- Continued comprehensive security performance, including effective security cooperation on the bases laid out in Phase I.

- Creation of an independent Palestinian state with provisional borders through a process of Israeli-Palestinian engagement, launched by the international conference. As part of this process, implementation of prior agreements, to enhance maximum territorial contiguity, including further action on settlements in conjunction with establishment of a Palestinian state with provisional borders.

- Enhanced international role in monitoring transition, with the active, sustained, and operational support of the Quartet.

- Quartet members promote international recognition of Palestinian state, including possible UN membership.

Phase III: Permanent Status Agreement and End of the Israeli-Palestinian Conflict—2004–2005

Progress into Phase III, based on consensus judgment of Quartet, and taking into account actions of both parties and Quartet monitoring. Phase III objectives are consolidation of reform and stabilization of Palestinian institutions, sustained, effective Palestinian security performance, and Israeli-Palestinian negotiations aimed at a permanent status agreement in 2005.

- **Second International Conference:** Convened by Quartet, in consultation with the parties, at beginning of 2004 to endorse agreement reached on an independent Palestinian state with provisional borders and formally to launch a process with the active, sustained, and operational support of the Quartet, leading to a final, permanent status resolution in 2005, including on borders, Jerusalem, refugees, settlements; and, to support progress toward a comprehensive Middle East settlement between Israel and Lebanon and Israel and Syria, to be achieved as soon as possible.

- Continued comprehensive, effective progress on the reform agenda laid out by the Task Force in preparation for final status agreement.

- Continued sustained and effective security performance, and sustained, effective security cooperation on the bases laid out in Phase I.

- International efforts to facilitate reform and stabilize Palestinian institutions and the Palestinian economy, in preparation for final status agreement.

- Parties reach final and comprehensive permanent status agreement that ends the Israel-Palestinian conflict in 2005, through a settlement negotiated between the parties based on UNSCR 242, 338, and 1397, that ends the occupation that began in 1967, and includes an agreed, just, fair, and realistic solution to the refugee issue, and a negotiated resolution on the status of Jerusalem that takes into account the political and religious concerns of both sides, and protects the religious interests of Jews, Christians, and Muslims world-wide, and fulfills the vision of two states, Israel and sovereign, independent, democratic and viable Palestine, living side-by-side in peace and security.

- Arab state acceptance of full normal relations with Israel and security for all the states of the region in the context of a comprehensive Arab-Israeli peace.

[End]
Released on April 30, 2003

ENDNOTES

Chapter 1:

1. Tim Llewellyn, "The Birth of Israel," *BBC Online Network*, 20 April 1998. http://news6.thdo.bbc.co.uk?hi/english/israel_at_50/history/newsid_78000/78601.stm: P. 1.

2. Thomas L. Friedman, *From Beirut To Jerusalem*, (New York: Farrar Straus Giroux, 1989), P. 14.

3. Llewellyn, "The Birth of Israel," p. 2.

4. United Nations, *History of the Palestinian Problem: Question of Palestine*. http://www.un.org/Depts/dpa/ngo/history.html: P. 1-3.

5. "Arab Israeli Wars History Text." http://members.nbci.com/_xmcm/palestine99/wartext.htm: P. 1-6.

6. Abdullah Frangi, "Palestinians Have A Right To A Homeland In Israel," in *The Middle East: Opposing Viewpoints*, ed. Janelle Rohr (St. Paul, Minnesota: Greenhaven Press, 1988), p. 137.

7. Tim Llewellyn, "Israel and the PLO," *BBC Online Network*, 20 April 1998. http://news6thdo.bbc.co./uk/hi/English/events/israel_at_50/history/newsid_78000/78655.stm: P. 1.

8. Friedman, *From Beirut To Jerusalem*, p. 108.

9. "Arab Israeli Wars History Text," p. 1-6.

10. United Nations, *History of the Palestinian Problem: Question of Palestine*, p. 2.

11. Ronald Stockton, "Teaching the Israeli-Palestinian Conflict," (Dearborn, Michigan: November 1993). http://www.umich.edu/~iinet/cmenas/StudyUnits/israeli-palestinianconflict/index.html.

12. Mark Perry, *A Fire In Zion: The Israeli-Palestinian Search For Peace* (New York: William Marrow and Company, 1994), p. 11.

13. Stockton, "Teaching the Israeli-Palestinian Conflict."

14. Phyllis Bennis, *From Stones To Statehood: The Palestinian Uprising* (New York: Olive Branch Press, 1989), P. 12

15. Friedman, *From Beirut To Jerusalem*, p. 413.

16. Bennis, *From Stones To Statehood: The Palestinian Uprising*, p. 12-13.

17. Bennis, *From Stones To Statehood: The Palestinian Uprising*, p. 44.

18. Ibid., P. 39.

19. Ibid., P. 82.

20. Friedman, *From Beirut To Jerusalem*, p. 421.

21. Mitchell Bard, "The Intifada," *The Jewish Student Online Research Center* (2001).

22. Columbia University Press, "Intifada," *The Columbia Electronic Encyclopedia* (2000). http://www.factmonster.com/co6/history/A0825375.

Chapter 2:

1. American-Israeli Cooperative Enterprise, "The Executive Branch," *Jewish Virtual Library*. http://www.us-israel.org/jsource/politics/exec_branch.html.

2. American-Israeli Cooperative Enterprise, "The Labor Party Platform," May 1997. http://www.us-israel.org/jsource/politics/labor.html.

3. Ibid.

4. Ibid.

5. Ibid.

6. "1999 Likud Party Platform," 29 April 1999. http://www.gamla.org.il/english/article/1999/april/ler2.htm.

7. Ibid.

8. Ibid.

9. Ibid.

10. "Yitzhak Rabin." http://www.ttt.org.il/nov/rabin.htm.

11. "The Path To Peace Runs Through A History of Turmoil," *CNN.com*. http://www.cnn.com/SPECIALS/2000/mideast/story/overview/: P. 1-6).

12. "Yitzhak Rabin." http://www.ttt.org.il/nov/rabin.htm.

13. "Al Mashriq—Interim Self Agreement Between Israel and the PLO,' *Israel Information Service Gopher* (September 1993). http://almashriq.hiof.no/ israel/300/320/327/interim-self-gov.html: P. 1 .

14. Ibid., P. 3.

15. Stockton, "Teaching the Israeli-Palestinian Conflict."

16. Yitzhak Rabin, "Israel Is Committed To Peace," in *Israel: Opposing Viewpoints* ed. Charles Cozic (San Diego: Greenhaven Press, Inc., 1994), p. 101.

17. Jonathan Parker, "Peace Hopes Buried." http://pages.ripco.net/~alderson/1/ jpnews.htm.

18. "Agreement on the Gaza Strip and Jericho Area," *Israel Information Service Gopher*, (4 May 1994). http://almashriq.hiof.no/general/300/320/ 327/gaza_and_jericho_00.html.

19. "Letter From Chairman Yasir Arafat to Prime Minister Rabin," 9 September 1993. http://www.palestine-un.org/peace/p_b.html.

20. Israeli Government Printing Office. 1997. *Palestinian Incitement To Violence Since Oslo: A Four-Year Compendum*: P. 1-16.

21. Israeli Government Printing Office. 1997. *Palestinian Incitement To Violence Since Oslo: A Four-Year Compendum*: P. 1.

22. Jonathan Parker, "Peace Hopes Buried." http://pages.ripco.net/~alderson/1/jpnews.htm).

23. National Alliance of Lebanese Americans, "The Passing of Yitzhak Rabin," 10 November 1995. http://www.nala.com/Editorial/RABIN.html: P. 1-3.

24. Ibid., p. 1-3.

25. "Shimon Peres: Winner of the 1994 Nobel Prize In Peace," *The Nobel Prize Internet Archive.* http://www.almaz.com/nobel/peace/1994b.html.

26. American-Israeli Cooperative Enterprise, "Shimon Peres."

27. "The Path To Peace Runs Through A History of Turmoil," *CNN.com*, p. 1-6.

28. Benjamin Netanyahu, "Palestinians Should Not Have Their Own Nation," in *Israel: Opposing Viewpoints* ed. Charles Cozic, (San Diego: Greenhaven Press, Inc., 1994), p. 153.

29. Ron Linser, "Role Profile: Benjamin Netanyahu, Israeli Prime Minister." *University of Melbourne.* http://ariel.ucs.unimelb.edu.au/~ronilins/WPT/Profiles/netanyahu.html.

30. American-Israeli Cooperative Enterprise, "The Labor Party Platform," May 1997. http://www.us-israel.org/jsource/politics/labor.html.

31. Benjamin Netanyahu. *A Durable Peace: Israel And Its Place Among The Nations.* (New York: Warner Books, 2000), p. 162.

32. "The Path To Peace Runs Through A History of Turmoil," *CNN.com*, p. 5).

33. ABC News, "Ehud Barak." http://www.abcnews.go.com/reference/bios/barak.html.

34. "The Path To Peace Runs Through A History of Turmoil," *CNN.com*, p. 1.

35. Dr. Mustafa Barghouti, "Why Palestinians Could Not Accept Barak's Proposal," *Arabic Media Internet Network.* http://www.amin.org/En/eyejrs/0105/free3_020501.html: P. 2.

36. Louis Gerber, "Ariel Sharon: Israel's New Prime Minister," *Cosmopolis*, February 2001. http://www.cosmopolis.ch/english/cosmo14/arielsharon.htm.

37. Elaine C. Hagopian, "The Pope's Emphasis on Palestinian Rights," *The Boston Globe*, 16 May 2001: P. A15.

38. Ibid.

39. Robert Malley and Hussein Agha, "Camp David: The Tragedy of Errors," *The New York Review*, 9 August 2001: P. 59.

40. Dr. Ron Pundak, "From Oslo To Taba: What Went Wrong," June 2001: P. 10.

41. Myre, "Departing U.S. Ambassador Faults Israelis, Palestinians," p. A7.

42. Keith Richburg, "The Palestinians' New Dilemma," *The Washington Post National Weekly Edition*, February 19-25, 2001: P. 12.

43. Rachelle Marshall, "Is Arafat To Blame For Sharon's Victory? Or Was Defeat 'Barak's and Barak's Alone?," *The Washington Report on Middle East Affairs*, April 2001, P. 6.

44. Rachelle Marshall, "Is Arafat To Blame For Sharon's Victory? Or Was Defeat 'Barak's and Barak's Alone?," p. 7.

45. Jane Adas. "Dr. Ghada Karmi, Prof. Lev Grinberg Analyze Post-Oslo Mideast," *Washington Report on Middle East Affairs,* Jan/Feb 2003, p. 56.

46. Tracy Wilkinson, "The Beginning of the End for Ehud Barak," *Los Angeles Times*, 1 December 2000.

47. "Peace Did Not Fail," *Uri Avnery*, (2001), http://www.gush-shalom.org/archives/article131.html.

48. Gerber, "Ariel Sharon: Israel's New Prime Minister," February 2001.

Chapter 3:

1. "The Path To Peace Runs Through A History of Turmoil," *CNN.com*, p. 1.

2. William Maclean, "Sharon To Stand Against Barak In Israel Polls," *Reuters* 29 November 2000. http://uk.news.yahoo.com/001129/80/aqfu7.html.

3. Ariel Sharon, "I Am For A Lasting Peace," November 14, 2000. http://www.freeman.org/m_online/dec00/sharon.htm.

4. Tore Kjeilen, *Encyclopedia of the Orient*, "Ariel Sharon." http://www.i.cias.com/e.o/sharon_ariel.htm: P. 1-2.

5. Gerald Butt, "Ariel Sharon: Controversial Hardliner," *BBC News* 7 February 2001.   http://news.bbc.co.uk/hi/english/world/middle_east/newsid_1154000/1154622.stm.

6. William Dankenbring, "A New Look At Ariel Sharon, 'Lion of God'—Man of Destiny?" *Triumph Prophetic Ministries*. http://hope-of-israel.org/sharon.htm: P. 2.

7. "Ariel Sharon: Peacemaker or Peace Breaker," *CNN.com*, 25 October 2000. http://www.cnn.com/2000/WORLD/meast/10/25/sharon.profile/.

8. Jeremy Salt, "Portrait of a Killer," *Arena Magazine*, December 1998, p. 8.

9. Butt, "Ariel Sharon: Controversial Hardliner," p. 2.

10. Kjeilen, "Ariel Sharon," p. 2.

11. Dankenbring, "A New Look At Ariel Sharon, 'Lion of God'—Man of Destiny?," p. 1-3.

12. Uzi Benziman, *Sharon: An Israeli Caesar*, (New York: Adama Books, 1985), p. 91.

13. Dankenbring, "A New Look At Ariel Sharon, 'Lion of God'—Man of Destiny?," p. 2-3.

14. Benziman, *Sharon: An Israeli Caesar*, p. 91-92.

15. Ariel Sharon with David Chanoff, *Warrior: An Autobiography* (New York: Simon & Schuster, 1989), p. 347.

16. Ariel Sharon with David Chanoff, *Warrior: An Autobiography*, p. 355.

17. Ibid., p. 365.

18. Ibid., p. 393.

19. Ibid., p. 402.

20. Benziman, *Sharon: An Israeli Caesar*, p. 225.

21. Ibid., p. 231.

22. Salt, "Portrait of a Killer," *Arena Magazine*, December 1998: P. 8.

23. Ariel Sharon with David Chanoff, *Warrior: An Autobiography*, p. 523.

24. Ibid., P. 527.

25. Benziman, *Sharon: An Israeli Caesar*, p. 235.

26. Ariel Sharon with David Chanoff, *Warrior: An Autobiography*, p. 345.

27. Ibid., P. 545-545.

28. Ibid., P. 545.

29. Ibid., P. 554.

30. Butt, "Ariel Sharon: Controversial Hardliner," p. 4.

31. "Ariel Sharon: Peacemaker or Peace Breaker?", *CNN.com* 25 October 2000. http://www.cnn.com/2000/WORLD/meast/10/25/shaton.profile/: P. 1-2.

32. Ibid., P. 2.

33. Ariel Sharon, "Still Fighting For Jerusalem." http://www.israel-embassy.org.uk/web/pages/jerushin.htm).

34. Ariel Sharon, "Why Should Israel Reward Syria?," *The New York Times*, 28 December 1999.

35. Friedman, *From Beirut To Jerusalem*, p. 268-269.

36. Kjeilen, "Ariel Sharon," p. 3.

37. "Ariel Sharon Wants To Annex Large Parts of West Bank to Protect Water," *Associated Press*, 21 May 1997.

38. "Ariel Sharon: Peacemaker or Peace Breaker," *CNN.com*, 25 October 2000.

39. "Ariel Sharon: Controversial Hardliner," *BBC News* 26 January 2001.

40. Stockton, "Teaching The Israeli-Palestinian Conflict."

41. Tarif Kafala, "Analysis: Is Sharon Coming or Going," *BBC News*, 27 April 2001.   http://news.bbc.co.uk/hi/english/world/middle_east/newsid.1285000/1285887.stm.

42. Ariel Sharon, "Our Pain Must Not Obscure Our Judgment," *The Jerusalem Post*, 16 November 1995. http://www.freeman.org/m_online/dec95/dec95e.htm.

43. Ariel Sharon, "The Likud's Plan, Simply Put," *The Jerusalem Post*, June 1996. http://www.freeman.org/m_online/jun96/sharon1.htm.

44. Ibid.

45. Ibid.

46. Butt, "Ariel Sharon: Controversial Hardliner," p. 3.

47. "Ariel Sharon: Peacemaker or Peace Breaker," *CNN.com*, 25 October 2000.

48. Ariel Sharon, "Leadership Equals Responsibility," *The Jerusalem Post* 3 March 2000. http://www.freeman.org/m_online/march00/sharon1.htm.

49. Ariel Sharon, "State In Turmoil," *The Jerusalem Post* 18 August 2000. http://www.freeman.org/m_online/sep00/sharon.html.

50. Ibid.

51. Ariel Sharon, "There's No Such Thing As A Free Lunch," *The Jerusalem Post* 21 February 2000. http://www.freeman.org/m_online/mar00/sharon3.htm.

52. Ariel Sharon, "Barak Is Outmaneuvered," *The Jerusalem Post* 4 February 2000. http://www.freeman.org/m_online/mar00/sharon2.htm.

53. Ariel Sharon, "Leadership Equals Responsibility." 3 March 2000.

54. "Ariel Sharon: Controversial Hardliner," *BBC News*, 26 January 2001. http://news.bbc.co.uk/hi/english/world/middle_east/newsid_190000/190257.stm.

55. Ariel Sharon, "Tell The Truth, Barak," February 2000. http://www.freeman.org/m_online/feb00/sharon2.html.

56. Ibid.

57. Ariel Sharon, "Six Red Lines For Peace," *The Jerusalem Post* 21 July 2000. http://www.freeman/org/m_online/aug00/ariel.htm.

58. Ibid.

59. "Ariel Sharon: Controversial Hardliner," BBC News, 26 January 2001.

60. Ariel Sharon, "Letter to Secretary of State Madeleine Albright," October 2, 2000. http://www.freeman.org/m_online/oct00/sharon.htm.

61. "Peace Did Not Fail," *Uri Avnery* 2001. http://www.gush-shalom.org/archives/article131.html.

62. "The Path To peace Runs Through A History of Turmoil." *CNN.com*, p. 1-2.

63. Hockstader, "A New Day In Israel," p. 17.

64. Richburg, "The Palestinians New Dilemma," p. 12.

65. Dan Ephron, "Cease-Fire Fading Fast In Mideast," *The Boston Globe*, 3 July 2001: P. A1.

66. Megan Goldin, "European Leaders At Odds With Sharon Stance," *The Boston Globe* 7 July 2001: P. A6.

67. Ibid.

68. Charles M. Sennott, "Court To Rule On The Role Of Sharon's Son," *The Boston Globe* 4 May 2001.

69. Ibid.

70. Larry Weymouth, "This Can't Go On," *Newsweek* 2 July 2001: P. 37.

71. Ibid., P. 38.

72. Ibid., P. 37-38.

73. "Sharon In His Own Words," *The Guardian*, 7 February 2001. http://guardianunlimited.co.uk/israel/story/0,2763,434618,00.html.

74. Larry Weymouth, "This Can't Go On," p. 38.

75. Charles Sennott, "Sharon Defiant on Settlements," *The Boston Globe* 9 May 2001: P. A1, A14.

76. Tarik Kafal, "Spotlight on Israeli Cabinet," *BBC News* 8 March 2001. http://news.bbc.co.uk/hi/english/world/middle_east/newsid_1209000/1209394.stm.

Chapter 4:

1.   "The Mitchell Report on the Mideast," *The Miami Herald*, 17 May 2000.

2.   Ibid.

3.   Ibid.

4.   Herb Keinon, "Israel Welcomes Mitchell Report," *The Jerusalem Post*, 22 May   2001.   http://www.jpost.com/Editions/2001/05/22/News/News.26707.html.

5.   "The Mitchell Report on the Mideast," *The Miami Herald*, 17 May 2000.

6.   Ibid.

7.   Ibid.

8.   Ibid.

9.   United Nations News Service, "Middle East: Annan Says Release of Mitchell Commission Report Offers Hope," 22 May 2001. http://www.un.org/News/dh/latest/page2.html#2.

10. Keinon, "Israel Welcomes Mitchell Report."

11. "Colin Powell's Comments on Mideast," *Associated Press*, 21 May 2001. Available: http://dailynews.yahoo.com/h/ap/20010521/w1/ powell_text_3.html.

12. Keinon, "Israel Welcomes Mitchell Report."

13. "Colin Powell's Comments on Mideast," *Associated Press*, 21 May 2001.

14. Keinon, "Israel Welcomes Mitchell Report."

15. Learning Network (2000), "The Gaza Strip," *The World & News.* http:// www.factmonster.com/ce6/world/A0858346: P. 2.

16. Tim Llewellyn, "The Birth of Israel," p. 4.

17. Larry Weymouth, "I Can Make Peace," *Newsweek*, 19 March 2001, P. 36-37.

18. Ibid.

19. Janet McMahon, "Facts For Your Files," *The Washington Report on Middle East Affairs,* April 2001, P. 55.

20. Lee Hockstader, "A New Day In Israel," p. 17.

21. Israeli Government Printing Office. 1997. *Palestinian Incitement To Violence Since Oslo: A Four-Year Compendum*, P. 1.

22. Ibid., P. 7.

23. Perry, *A Fire In Zion: The Israeli-Palestinian Search For Peace*, p. 223.

24. "Mideast Inaction," [Editorial] *The Boston Globe*, 10 July 2001: P. A18.

25. Ibid.

26. Ibid.

27. Jeff Halper, "Sharon's National Unity Government: Shoring Up The 'Iron Wall,'" *MERIP Press Information News Note 50*, 13 March 2001: P. 1.

28. Jeff Halper, "Sharon's National Unity Government: Shoring Up The 'Iron Wall,'" p. 3.

29. Joshua Hammer, "Israel's Unpluggable Palestinian Problem," *Newsweek*, 19 March 2001: P. 38.

30. Dan Ephron, "Israeli Tanks Raid Palestinian Camp," *The Boston Globe*, 12 April 2001.

31. Ibid.

32. Elena Becatoros, "Amid the Violence, Israelis and Palestinians Hold Talks," *The Boston Globe*, 5 April 2001, P. A13.

33. Hussein Ibish, "Despite the Bombing of Baghdad, Powell Mideast Tour Signals Hope For More Balanced U.S. Policy In Region," *The Washington Report on Middle East Affairs*, April 2001, p. 21.

34. Dan Ephron, "U.S. Policy in Israel Viewed As Unfair," *The Boston Globe*, 5 April 2001.

35. Elena Becatoros, "Amid the Violence, Israelis and Palestinians Hold Talks," p. A13.

36. Jonathan Wright, "Israel Seeks Reduced US Role In Mideast Talks," *The Boston Globe*, 3 May 2001, p. A18.

37. Greg Myre, "Departing U.S. Ambassador Faults Israelis, Palestinians," p. A7.

38. Dan Ephron, "U.S. Brokers A Cease-Fire In Mideast," *The Boston Globe*, 13 June 2001, P. A1, A26.

39. Larry Weymouth, "This Can't Go On," p. 38.

40. Greg Myre, "Departing U.S. Ambassador Faults Israelis, Palestinians," *The Boston Globe*, 5 July 2001, p. A7.

41. Chris Hawley, "U.S. Vetoes U.N. Resolution Backing An Observer Force For Palestinians," *The Lowell Sun*, 28 March 2001, p. 3.

42. Charles Sennott, "Sharon Defiant on Settlements," *The Boston Globe*, 9 May 2001, p. A1.

43. Ibid.

44. Dan Ephron, "Israel Destroys Refugee Homes," *The Boston Globe*, 10 July 2001.

45. Elaine C. Hagopian, "The Pope's Emphasis on Palestinian Rights," p. A15.

46. Mark Lavie, "Sharon Rejects Israeli-Arafat Talks," *The Boston Globe*, 18 June 2001.

47. Dan Perry, "Israelis Consider Military Invasion," *Associated Press*, 14 July 2001.

Chapter 5

1. Stockton, "Teaching The Israeli-Palestinian Conflict."

2. Palestinefacts.org, "Israel 1991 to Present PA Corruption."

3. Greg Myre. "Sharon Rebuffs Arafat's Offer To Meet Immediately and Resume Talks," *Associated Press*, January 29, 2003.

4. Dan Perry, "Sharon Wins A Crushing Victory Over Labor," *Associated Press*, January 29, 2003.

5. Greg Myre. "Sharon Rebuffs Arafat's Offer To Meet Immediately and Resume Talks," *Associate Press*, January 29, 2003.

6. Associated Press, "Sharon Dismisses Quartet Peace Plan," 19 January 2003.

7. Kevin Laub, "Israel OK's Peace Plan," *Associated P*ress, 26 May 2003.

8. Mark Lavie, "Sharon's Conciliatory Tone Shocks Israel's Hawks," *Associated Press*, 27 May 2003.

9. Kevin Laub, "Israel OK's Peace Plan," *Associated P*ress, 26 May 2003.

10. Ibid.

Conclusion:

1.   "Groundbreaking Survey of U.S. Jews and Arabs," *The Washington Report on Middle East Affairs*, January/February 2003, p. 69.

"The Oslo agreement is finished. It doesn't exist."

—Ariel Sharon, January 2001

The May 22, 2001 *Frankfurter Rundschow* of Germany observed, "Never since the Oslo Peace Accords has war seemed so likely." In this fast-paced, well-researched, and thoroughly-documented work, author Dennis "D.J." Deeb II objectively traces the rise and fall of the Oslo Peace Accords between the Israelis and Palestinians. What went wrong with peace? Deeb discusses the policies followed by the Israeli government and Palestinian Authority since the signing of the Oslo Accords in 1993 up through the election of controversial Israeli Prime Minister Ariel Sharon, who is opposed to the Oslo Peace Accords. This work also analyzes Sharon's statements and past record as a military and government leader with regards to the Peace Process. Deeb also discusses the corruption within the Palestinian Authority that have hindered the peace process, including the mismanagement of Palestinian Authority President Yasir Arafat. The author examines and supports what has become known as "The Mitchell Report," released in the spring 2001, in offering a lasting peace between Israelis and Palestinians. He also considers and evaluates the recent Road Map To Peace proposal offered by President George W. Bush in the spring of 2003. Since 1993, both Israeli and Palestinian leaders have failed to implement and have violated provisions of the Oslo Accords. As the late Israeli Prime Minister Yitzhak Rabin, who gave his life in the name of peace, and to whom this writing is dedicated, articulated so clearly during the signing of the Oslo Accords, "enough blood and tears." Finally, Deeb argues that the intent behind the Oslo Accords encompass the link between the end of war and the era of peace, that the Israelis and Palestinians should both return to the table for negotiations based upon the recommendations of "The Mitchell Report" and the Quartet Road Map To Peace to negotiate a final and lasting settlement rooted in the Oslo Peace Accords.

BIBLIOGRAPHY (RECOMMENDED READING)

Bennis, Phyllis *From Stones To Statehood: The Palestinian Uprising*. New York: Olive Branch Press, 1989.

Friedman, Thomas. *From Beirut To Jerusalem*. New York: Farrar, Straus and Giroux, 1989.

Netanyahu, Benjamin. *A Durable Peace: Israel And Its Place Among The Nations*. New York: Warner Books, 2000.

Perry, Mark. *A Fire In Zion: The Israeli-Palestinian Search For Peace*. New York: William Marrow and Company, 1994.

Sharon, Ariel with David Chanoff. *Warrior: The Autobiography of Ariel Sharon*. New York: Simon and Schuster, 1989.

Thomas, Baylis. *How Israel Was Won: A Concise History of the Arab-Israeli Conflict*. Lanham, Maryland: Lexington Books, 1999.

ABOUT THE AUTHOR

Dennis "D.J." Deeb II is a resident of Dracut, Massachusetts, where he has served as an elected official since 1997. He has been a History/Humanities teacher at Reading Memorial High School in Reading, Massachusetts since 2001. He also works as an adjunct History/Government instructor at Northern Essex Community College in Haverhill, Massachusetts.

0-595-29770-6